Beyond the Skills and Drills:

The Keys to Successfully Coaching Youth Sports

Coaching at the Youth Level, based on these
highly effective online programs,
Coaching to Make a Positive Difference
Looking in the Mirror
Positive Parent Participation

Every Youth Coach in America needs
to read and absorb this book.

www.coaching-coaches.com

Bill Bommarito

Coaching Coaches
Beyond the Skills and Drills:
The Keys to Successfully Coaching Youth Sports

© 2023 by Bill Bommarito

ISBN: 978-1-63110-545-6

Printed in the United States of America by
Graphic Connections Group Publishing
Chesterfield, Missouri 63005

Testimonials

"A must read for coaches and parents in youth sports. Bill Bommarito inspires you to do your best. Coaching with Bill taught me about preparation, the importance of building a program, and how to communicate to ensure youth athletes and their parents feel that they are a vital part of the team. Most of all, Bill helped me understand the role of coaches in youth sports and how as a coach we can provide a positive experience as we help children develop into successful adults."

Allan Crean, Volunteer Coach
Director, Computer Education & Training Center,
University of Missouri – St. Louis
Total number of years involved in youth sports: 16 years

"Want to be a great coach for your players and parents? Absorb Bill Bommarito's wisdom-infused book about coaching with heart! His insightful knowledge and people-centered teachings celebrate the player-coach connection, encourage caring deeply about each athlete, and guides coaches in growing each team member to be their best selves. Bill's book and insight is game-changing and a gift to all who love sports and the future of our kids."

Mary Sly, Vice President, #KeeleyCares
Assistant Soccer Coach with Bill for 4 years
Total number of years involved in youth sports: 10 years

"Read this book, please! When Bill Bommarito talks about coaching young people, we all need to listen. His approach, methods, and standards are at the top of the class. This is what I know: bringing Bill Bommarito and his programs to the St. Louis CYC Sports program has had a lasting positive effect on our coaches, parents, and youth participants."

Mike Kalist, Director of the Catholic Youth Council (Archdiocese of St. Louis)
Director, 1985 – 2007
Total number of years involved in youth sports: 53 years

"Bill is the best preacher-teacher-mentor and 'Coach of coaches' I've ever met. And in 40 years of high school coaching, teaching, and thinking about how to help young people grow, I've met a lot of them. If you love sports and believe in what sports can do for our youth, you no doubt also know that for all the money, time, and energy we're investing, youth sports are in trouble today. Bill has the diagnosis, and this book will help you find the cure. Not only will he help you get organized and run a program that builds individual skills and creates a positive and enjoyable sporting environment, but you'll learn how to keep your energy and skill as a coach firmly rooted where your heart truly is: helping our kids and our teams to become the best possible versions of themselves."
Jim Linhares, Assistant Principal for Mission
St. Louis University High School, St. Louis, MO
Head Cross Country Coach/Head Track Coach
2010, Hall of Fame Inductee into the Missouri Track and
Cross Country Coaches Association
Total number of years involved in youth sports: 40 years

"Bill Bommarito and his program not only helped my development as a coach, but it guided me to focus on the relationships needed to run a successful program. You will be missing out as a coach and as a director of youth sports if you do not read this book."
Jeremy Jones, International Sports Missionary
Former High School Basketball Coach and
Youth Basketball Director and Coach
Total number of years involved in youth sports: 15 years

"Is this your first coaching experience? Have you coached teams before? If you answered 'yes' to either question, THIS BOOK IS FOR YOU! This book gives you exactly what every youth coach should know, and it tells you how to apply that information at practices and games. Once our organization's coaches used Bill's tools, I was confident they would provide our girls and boys a great and fun sports experience. Please read the book and do the same for your team."
Buzz Swanston, Assistant Sports Director, CYC
(Archdiocese of St. Louis)
Total number of years involved in youth sports: 55 years

"As the St. Louis CYC Sports Director for over 30 years, I have known Bill Bommarito for over 25 years as a parent, a coach, an athletic association president, a presenter, and as a developer of Coaching and Parent Programs. Bill was excellent in all his positions, but with the Coaching and Parent Programs, he took it to another level. He has trained thousands of coaches and parents within our program. Entertaining, engaging, and down-to-earth are just a few words to describe the programs that he has developed and presented, both in person and online. His involvement in our program, which averaged over 5,000 teams and 75,000 participants annually, was a major plus for bringing our coaches and parents to a higher standard. This book is a must read for both new coaches and experienced coaches."
Paul Scovill, CYC Sports Director (Archdiocese of St. Louis)
High School Boys' Varsity Volleyball Coach and
High School Volleyball Official
Total number of years involved in youth sports: 47 years

"Bill Bommarito has been a professional associate and friend of mine for over 40 years. His positive teaching talents and powerful perspectives on youth sports are invaluable resources for athletes, coaches, parents, and athletic administrators at all levels. His methods and views are appropriate for any sport, and he has shared his dynamic ideas with thousands of coaches in multiple courses in his *Coaching Coaches* program. Whether you are a first-time coach or a seasoned veteran, this book will be a priceless resource in your coaching and teaching library. I have no doubt that you will put what you learn from Bill to practical use as a coach, athlete, parent, or community leader. Good luck, and enjoy the read."
James M. Siewe, CLU, ChFC
High School Head Football Coach in Ohio
Additional Youth Coaching, Administration, Booster VP/President, and HOF Selection Committee
Total number of years involved in youth sports: 54 years

Contents

Dedication/Acknowledgments

I wish to dedicate this book to my wife, Margaret.
She has sacrificed a great deal to help me pursue my passion.
I thank you and love you!

In addition, I wish to thank my daughters, Lauren, Molly,
and Amy, and their families for their constant love and
unconditional support of my dreams.
I thank you and love all of you!

I also wish to acknowledge and thank my extended family and
in particular my brother Larry who, for years, has supported
and helped me with my dreams, ambitions, computer, writing,
and my endless phrase, "But can we do it this way?"
With great love, thanks to all of you.

I also want to acknowledge and thank all the coaches,
administrators, and officials, I have had the pleasure to
coach with, work with, and learn from as I honed my skills
and developed a philosophy of coaching. I have been
blessed to be a part of your lives and your work ethic.
I thank every one of you!

Finally, I wish to thank past, present and future coaches
and parents who will take the time to read and absorb
this book and its philosophy of coaching.
To move the needle in a positive direction takes all
of us understanding the real reasons we teach and
coach at this level. (Hint: It is not to win!)
Enjoy the opportunity to make a significant and
positive difference in a child's life!
Thank you, youth coaches and parents!

Foreword

I really want you to read this book, which is why I consented to write the foreword. And it's not just for the typical reasons (fame and fortune and adulation, and maybe some others). I want you to read this because I am convinced that you will benefit from it. You'll be a better coach for sure, but you'll also be a better person for getting to know Bill Bommarito, who brings a missionary's zeal to his work of making not just better coaches, but better people. Trust me--you'll thank me when you're finished.

A good foreword should personally recommend the text, enlighten the reader about the bona fides of the author, and lead you gently but excitedly into the author's world. I can do all of that and then some in recommending Bill Bommarito's book, *Beyond the Skills and Drills: The Keys to Successfully Coaching Youth Sports*.

Bill Bommarito is a coach's coach—he was born to coach. Blessed with a high level of athletic talent, he was exposed to most of the sports that many of us were privileged to play as kids (though most of us didn't know or appreciate it; our parents mostly wanted us out of the house). Bill didn't just play baseball and soccer and football and hockey—he absorbed it. He thought about strategy and not simply the next play; he saw the entire playing field and not just his position; he viewed his mates as parts of a team whole and not just as buddies on the roster. In short, he played the games with more than a young athlete's attitude. He was a player to be sure, and a good one at that, but he also began to view sports through a coach's lens, learning and appreciating sports at a strategic, tactical, and team level. In fact, at the age of 13, he was calling all the offensive plays for his junior football team. It soon became clear to Bill, even as a teenager, that coaching is what he wanted to do with his life.

So, it came as no surprise that after graduating from college, Bill taught and coached for several years at the high school level. Even as a 20-year-old, Bill was laying the groundwork for Coaching Coaches. Once his own kids were of age, Bill coached for many years at the volunteer level. His teams enjoyed a high level of success on the scoreboard, and he and his squads enjoyed the spoils of team victory and championships. The kids he coached were not only competitive, but they also enjoyed the process of Bill's program. Under his direction, Bill's players' sporting experience was not burdensome, but rather was exciting, as they learned about doing your best for yourself and your teammates. At a time when being a coach implied lots of yelling and demands, Bill took a different approach, and the kids responded with not only hard work and dedication, but also a sense of ownership, pride, and viewing their participation from a team perspective as opposed to an individual pursuit.

But Bill, ever the innovator and improver, sought more. He came to understand (or maybe he knew all along) that team sports were so much more than scoreboard watching and trophy hunting. He knew that the virtues that informed his personal life, virtues like integrity, hard work, preparation, attentiveness, perseverance, and finding the joy, could be communicated and strengthened by coaches who saw the opportunities for personal growth built into youth sports.

Coaches like Bill who embraced this approach to their teams and their young athletes came to view their roles much more broadly than those who sought only to maximize scoreboard wins. In this more holistic view, coaches could instruct young athletes, yes, but they could also mentor them, model mature behavior, emphasize collaboration and team goals, celebrate wins large and small, and have fun in the process. In short, Bill saw the need and opportunity to help transform young people into healthy, whole, and productive adults through the fun and joy of spirited athletic competition.

After many years of coaching at various levels, Bill's response to this important revelation led to his decision to establish Coaching Coaches for coaches nationwide. This company, which seeks to impart coaching wisdom and support for youth coaches, is not simply a job for Bill; it is his passion, his singular professional goal, and his dream to provide youngsters with a wonderful, healthy, and memorable sports experience that is facilitated by wise, caring, and generous coaches who demonstrate life lessons along with athletic knowledge.

Read this book. Enjoy the coaching anecdotes. Study and implement the Coaching Pyramid. But perhaps most of all, lean into the privilege and responsibility of coaching our youngsters and know that you can positively affect them while they are batting, kicking, skating, or defending. Coaching is an activity, but you have the opportunity to make it so much more. Bill Bommarito will take you there with experience, enthusiasm, and energy, so let's get started.

By the way, I am Bill's older brother, which is why I know so much of his story. He's the real deal, and if you can't get him to show up at one of your practices, *Beyond the Skills and Drills: The Keys to Successfully Coaching Youth Sports* is the next best thing. Enjoy the game, Coach!

–Larry Bommarito

Introduction

INTRODUCTION (Thank you for coaching!!)

Welcome to coaching! First, I want to thank each of you for your willingness to offer your time and talent to coach at the youth level. Coaching at the youth level can be both exhilarating and frustrating. I have walked the walk, and I can assure you that coaching at this level is much more fun than frustrating. However, the level of fun versus frustration is directly tied to your ability to prepare as if you are stepping into a classroom with motivational posters on the walls, welcoming signs, a big whiteboard, and 10 to 15 kids sitting in seats looking at you and wondering what kind of experience this is going to be.

Let's get this straight from the start: You are a TEACHER first and foremost and a COACH second. Our shirts should read *Teacher* and not *Coach* on the left label side of the shirt. Keep repeating to yourself that you are a teacher and not a paid coach. That simple concept changes everything. It changes how we view our role and the expectations of everyone involved. Not one of you will be retained from year to year based on your win/loss record. However, some of you may be asked to turn in your whistle if your focus is too much on the scoreboard and not so much on being a teacher and creating an environment that keeps the kids and parents coming back year after year. How you approach this volunteerism is almost entirely up to you. Take your role seriously. You have 10 to 15 kids and their parents looking to you to create this wonderful sporting experience. How will you measure up? Again, thank you so much for saying "yes" to teaching/coaching our kids. Settle in, welcome to the world of youth sports, and let's begin with my story.

At the age of 16, and inspired by my high school football coaches Don Heeb and Jim Farrell, I knew that I wanted to teach and coach at the high school level. Quite honestly, the *teaching* part was a necessary evil. I wanted to *coach* football and any other sport available to me. When I graduated from college, the only way to *coach* was to be hired as a classroom teacher at a public or private school. Therefore, I had to *teach* traditional classroom courses, which in my case were *business* classes. What a drag. I had to *teach* six to seven hours a day before I could go to practice and *coach*!

And guess what? A funny thing happened to me on the way to the practice field. I fell in love with the classroom! I loved the classroom, and I loved teaching. A second revelation occurred to me shortly thereafter. I discovered that as I became a better *teacher*, I became a much better coach. It dawned on me quickly that *coaching* is *teaching*! In addition, I discovered that if I wanted to be the best possible coach, I needed to continually improve my teaching skills.

I started to change my coaching approach to one of a highly prepared classroom. The field became an extension of my indoor classroom. I prepared as much for a practice as I did for a lesson in accounting. I didn't phone it in. I didn't think I knew everything about a given sport. I didn't think, "I played this sport, so I know more than anyone out here." I didn't treat any coaching assignment as if it was secondary to my "real" teaching gig. No, whatever team I was coaching got 100% of me—no different than the students in my business classes. What I discovered early in my career was simple: Effective teaching is a hard-won skill; effective coaching is equally difficult, and to be a good teacher or a good coach, you had to approach both classrooms with your best all the time.

There are times in the volunteer coaching world (K thru 10th grade) that a coach has been busy at home and busy at work and the practice prep or the game prep is done while driving to the practice or the game. That can't happen. I realize what you have so graciously signed up for is a nonpaid opportunity to be with your child and do the best you can. I get it. I did the exact same thing for many years; that is, I too was a volunteer coach. However, I had the benefit of teaching and coaching at a higher level as a full-time job, and what I hope to share with you are the benefits of approaching any volunteer commitment with doing a little more than the minimum. If you do a little more than the minimum, you will stand out like a superstar. If you effectively follow the suggestions of this book, you will have kids and parents running to sign up for your team next year because of these two pillars of coaching: **WHO you are (your character)** and **HOW you deliver your program**. If you are a quality person and you deliver an over-the-top good program, you will positively affect more lives than you ever thought possible. Be that coach who *gets it.*

Volunteer coaching at the grade school/high school level is *not* about you and what you know. It is your ability to take whatever knowledge you have and effectively share that knowledge with 10 or 15 kids and their parents. How you *deliver* your program will stay with these kids and their families for a lifetime. If it is a good experience for everyone, that will be remembered forever. If it is *not* a good experience for everyone, that too will be remembered forever. Bottom line, those memories are completely up to you!

Typically, at the grade school level (K thru 8th grade), there are no formal athletic directors who will walk you through what it means to coach young kids. Ms. or Mr. Volunteer Coach, it will be up to you to create your own program, and that is not an easy task. That is why I will constantly thank you for coaching our kids. You are heroes in my book!

Prior to the start of any season, I believe you must do some soul searching. Why are you coaching? What do you hope to achieve? What are your priorities? How important is *winning* to you and your assistant coaches? The list can go on and on. These questions and more should be answered prior to any season. And, if you cannot fully answer a question or two, you must at least have given it some thought. What will be your *best* when you make that first contact with your team and their parents?

Having listed those questions above, let's get the following on the table right now in the introduction: WINNING. How important is it to you? Does it drive your everyday life or your business life or your family life? Does your personality change as you compete at work or at recreational activities? Are you driven by winning? Regardless of how you answered the above questions, let me go on record and say WINNING is not a bad thing. We all want to win in our private lives, creating strong and healthy relationships. We all want to win in our business lives; we want to excel at work and be recognized for that effort. We all want to win in our recreational lives or, at least, compete well. WINNING is not a bad thing! However, I believe that any level of sport below high school varsity is NOT about WINNING. WINNING should NOT be our number one goal at the youth level.

I will also be so bold as to say, if you want to coach at the youth level and WINNING *is* your number one goal, I would ask you to NOT coach at this level. Go coach at the varsity high school level or the college level or the professional level. Starting at the varsity level of high school sports, coaches can lose their job if they do not win enough. We have all seen it happen. And, of course, we see that happen at the college level and the professional level.

My point is simple: WINNING must *not* be the number one objective of a youth coach. TEACHING is your first and foremost objective at this level. If you win because your kids are better taught (coached) and execute your well-thought-out practices to the level that creates "wins," so be it. That winning is a cherry on top. The secret here is, don't get caught up on winning. Get focused on teaching and becoming a better teacher every time you are with your kids. I believe our goal every year is to create the best sporting experience possible. If your players get your best at every practice and game because you are highly organized and focused on each child's development, you are already winning with every child and their parents.

Teach, teach, teach. Become the best possible teacher and, regardless of what the scoreboard says on game days, you will be winning where it counts: with the kids and their parents! The reason I focus on effective teaching is simple: If your focus is only on the scoreboard on game days, you will be disappointed. Why? As effective teachers, we are running a marathon and not a sprint. The goal is to have EVERY child come out year after year because of WHO you are and HOW you deliver your program. I can assure you this: If a child quits your team because of WHO you are or HOW you deliver your program, you will not be able to teach them anything going forward. Why? They won't be there!!

Coaches, in this book, I am going to ask a lot of you. For years, many organizations have tiptoed around volunteer coaches' training because the organizational leaders did not want to upset a coach for fear they may quit. To me, that is a fear-based strategy that lowers the bar for everyone. I want to raise the bar to provide our kids and their parents with the best volunteer coaches who understand what the true objectives are for this level of sport.

Remember, it is not WINNING, it is effective TEACHING over time (years) that has the most positive effect on your players. Coaching is teaching. Raise the bar for yourself, and if you need to adjust your priorities, please do so.

This book is structured like a sports season timeline: Preseason, In-Season, and Postseason. Every phase of a season is outlined for you. You may want to think of this book as a recipe book. What is needed to effectively prepare for your season? What is needed during the season to become the most effective teacher possible? Finally, what is needed after the season to assess your strengths and weaknesses and begin to focus on the next season?

Once again, I want to thank you for saying "yes" to coaching our kids! The first step of any process is simply making that commitment: "Yes, I will be the head coach or an assistant coach." As difficult as that decision may have been, it is the easiest part of the process of effectively coaching kids. The more challenging part of coaching is to effectively prepare for each phase of the season: preseason, in-season, and postseason. And finally, the most important part of youth coaching is to effectively and consistently enhance your teaching skills so that you create the best possible sporting experience for our kids, our parents, the game officials, the administration leadership, and yourself. Coaching always comes down to two things: **WHO you are** and **HOW you deliver your program!**

Many of you have seen the streaming program, Ted Lasso. In season one, episode three, Ted is having a conversation with sports reporter, Trent Crimm and Ted says, "I love coaching...for me, success is not about the wins and losses. It is about helping these young fellows be the best versions of themselves on and off the field." Ted, I could not have said it any better!

Let's get started!

Chapter 1

Coaching Coaches' Process Pyramid

Coaching Coaches' Process Pyramid

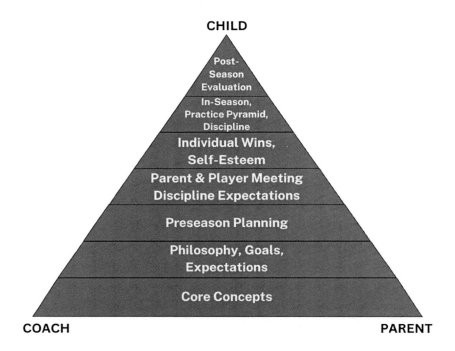

THE COACHING PYRAMID: The Coaching Coaches program is structured in a pyramid format. I find that it gives context to the breadth of the program. You will hear of very successful coaches using their "process" to be successful. Among football coaches, Nick Saban and Bill Belichick are probably the two best-known coaches renowned for developing and sticking to a process of coaching and of delivering their program. I too am a strong believer in embracing process. I have incorporated the concept of process for some 45 years. The Coaching Pyramid is a good example of using a process to achieve your end goals. (Side note: Before you start critiquing Coach Saban's and Coach Belichick's sideline coaching styles, remember that they are coaching at the college and professional level and not at the youth level.)

First, we start with the pyramid itself. The pyramid not only outlines the direction of your upcoming season, but it also shapes the building blocks associated with a well-planned season.

Let's start with the three points of the pyramid: Child, Coach, and Parent. These three groups must all understand what will be happening over the course of the season. A successful season depends on all three of these entities working together. Remember, that encompasses preseason, in-season, and postseason... and it all starts with YOU, the coach!

Most coaches get along with the kids, but many coaches keep the parents at arm's length. Many coaches even view the parents as the possible enemy or a necessary evil. That approach can completely undermine your program.

Many coaches say they went into coaching because they wanted to coach and work with the kids and NOT have to deal with the parents. This is dangerously shortsighted. As a volunteer coach, you must engage the parents to the same degree you engage the kids. The parents can help you build a successful program, or they can keep you from building the best possible program. Whether you like it or not, the parents at the youth level are very much part of the program. Therefore, educate them. Embrace them. Get them on your side. Make sure they understand your program and make sure they understand *their role* in your program!

The relationship between the coach and the kids is a given. Coaches typically want the opportunity to work with the kids. Treat the parents the same way. As a coach, you will not be working with the parents in the same way you work with the kids, but realize that the parents can help you or they can negatively impact your program.

What do you want for your program? Buy into the pyramid: Child, Coach, and Parent. Later in the book, I will detail the many ways in which you can bring the parents into your program as a huge supporter of your goals and mission. Remember that much will be asked of you as you take on this most important role of coach for your child and many other children and families! Effective TEACHING is effective COACHING whether you are working with the kids or the parents!

CORE CONCEPTS: I focus on four Core Concepts specific to youth coaching: 1) How you define your role as a volunteer coach; 2) A review of the Michigan State University study on youth sports; 3) The concept of Yelling vs. Teaching; and 4) Self-esteem techniques for effective teachers. See Chapter 2

PHILOSOPHY, GOALS, AND EXPECTATIONS: Well-thought-out philosophy, goals, and expectations will set the tone for your upcoming season. This section will help keep your program on track with your kids, your parents, and yourself! I will go into detail about Philosophy, Goals, and Expectations in Chapter 3.

PRESEASON PLANNING: Preseason planning is primarily forming your timetable and the details of your upcoming season. This process of effectively preparing for your upcoming season includes your first contact with the kids and their parents. Your first contact must be your best contact. The kids you will coach and their parents get their first opinion of who you are with that first contact. This important first contact is very much a part of your preseason preparation. Make it a good one! See Chapter 4

PARENT AND PLAYER MEETING (DISCIPLINE EXPECTATIONS): After you have developed your Philosophy, Goals and Expectations and you have incorporated those details into your Preseason Planning, you now must effectively deliver that information to the kids and their parents. Here is a little secret: Many coaches hate this section. Why? As discussed earlier, many coaches do not want to reach out to the parents. Given a choice, these coaches do not want the parents at their practices, and if possible, they would rather not have the parents at their games. I know that sounds ridiculous, but some coaches find the parents a necessary evil.

Please do not think that way. The parents make up one-third of your program. Bring them along the journey in a way that allows you to control the narrative. And there is no better way to do that than by conducting a parent/player meeting where you are in complete control. You get to lay out your vision, and if you do it in a professional and respectful manner, the parents (and the kids) will sit up a little taller, take notice, and feel good about being a part of something special—your team! I will go into far more detail when I address the specifics of a Parent/Player Meeting in Chapter 5. It is essential to any quality program.

INDIVIDUAL WINS AND SELF-ESTEEM: I put this section into the Coaching Pyramid because it must be a part of every quality program. I developed *Individual Wins* to highlight a teaching technique whereby you don't focus on the results but rather on the process. Hundreds of Individual Wins take place at every practice and game, and our role as coaches is to reward those Individual Wins as best we can. Knowing that not every child is a true athlete, it is a great way to boost everyone's contributions regardless of the outcome of a given play. We will discuss this in more detail in Chapter 6.

IN-SEASON, PRACTICE PYRAMID, AND DISCIPLINE: This part of the pyramid highlights the specifics necessary to communicate effectively, organize and conduct highly efficient practices, make everyone feel welcomed, and provides effective techniques for handling disruptions of your practices and/or games. No one can be an effective and successful teacher if they do not have control of their practice or game (their classroom!). Discipline is so much more effective when the consequences are known by everyone, including the parents, and dealt with in a low-key manner. We will talk more about the specifics in Chapter 7.

POSTSEASON EVALUATION: Every season has a beginning and an end. Unfortunately, in today's world, all the extracurricular activities seem to run together and, in many cases, overlap. Consequently, there is little or no time to assess what just happened over the last 90 to 120 days. How did the season go for the kids? How did the season go for their parents? How did the season go for YOU? I believe the postseason evaluation is every bit as important as any other part of the pyramid. This is the time that an effective coach assesses her/his performance. What went well this season? What did not go well this season? Did the kids and parents enjoy the sporting experience? There are dozens of questions you can answer that will immediately help you build an even better program for next year.

Remember, at this level of coaching, typically no one is available to assess your strengths and weaknesses. It is completely up to you. This step is very much part of the "process." Treat this part of the pyramid with as much enthusiasm as you would treat any other part of the Coaching Pyramid. More details will be available to you in Chapter 8.

Chapter 2

Core Concepts

Coaching Coaches' Process Pyramid — Core Concepts

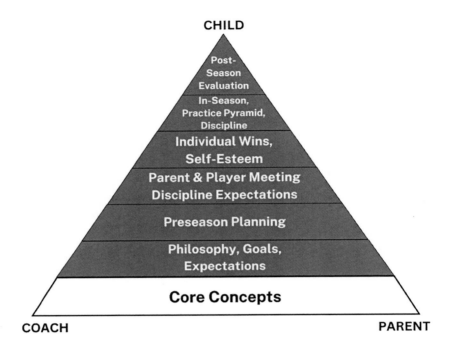

CHILD

Post-Season Evaluation

In-Season, Practice Pyramid, Discipline

Individual Wins, Self-Esteem

Parent & Player Meeting Discipline Expectations

Preseason Planning

Philosophy, Goals, Expectations

Core Concepts

COACH   PARENT

CORE CONCEPTS: I focus on four Core Concepts specific to youth coaching: 1) How you define your role as a volunteer coach; 2) A review of the Michigan State University study on youth sports; 3) The concept of Yelling vs. Teaching; and 4) Self-esteem techniques for effective teachers.

Core Concept Number One: Define Your Role as a Volunteer Coach: What is your role as a youth coach? How do YOU define your role as a volunteer coach? If someone was interviewing you right now and asked you the following question, how would you answer it: **"Coach, now that you have signed up to coach these kids, how would you define your role as 'Coach' with these (first graders or fifth graders or eighth graders or high schoolers)?"** Imagine yourself answering the question with a microphone pointed at you and some bright lights making you sweat a little. That answer should flow out of you like giving your name and address. That is, you know the answer because you have thought about it and have prepared yourself long before someone asked you this question.

But relax! No one is going to ask you this question. However, would an answer have poured out of you? Do you know the answer? Have you given that specific question some thought? It is step one to coaching/teaching our kids. Remember, especially at this level, EVERYTHING starts with YOU!

Define Your Role as a Coach

How do you **define** your role as a volunteer coach?

_____

_____

_____

_____

Redefining your role

You may consider **redefining** your role with some or all of the following:

- **The best coaches prove to be the best teachers.**
- **Effective coaches are teachers.**

  - *Erudio* (Latin) — to teach; to instruct; to educate
  - *Facio* (Latin) — to sacrifice; to help; **to be of service**
  - *Erudio/Facio* is to be **the coach you want to be.**

- Our job is to be a strong role model.
- Keep our kids in the shadow of a healthy environment.
- Treat our kids, their parents, fans, officials, the other teams, our administrators, and anyone else the way **you would want to be treated.**
- Become a positive ambassador for your organization, your community, and your family.

Because of the above: Coaching is truly a gift that you can share with every child and family you encounter during your coaching career. That should make you feel good! I sure hope it does! Thank you so much for coaching our kids!

Core Concept Number Two: A review of the Michigan State University Study on Youth Sports: The MSU study is detailed in the upcoming pages. The bottom line is this: What you may have thought about how kids would answer certain questions about youth sports becomes a real eye-opener for most coaches. Take a serious look at the kids' responses. It will have an impact on your coaching!

What Kids Tell Us about Youth Sports— Michigan State University Study

NOTE: I will be up-front with you about this study. This study is dated, but the authors believe that these answers would not change dramatically, based on other work that they do in the arena of youth sports. In fact, they believe that a similar study today would reinforce their findings.

The following information comes from a Michigan State University study of 10,000 kids from 11 cities, and their responses to several questions concerning youth sports. The study was conducted by Martha E. Ewing and Vern Seefeldt of the Youth Sports Institute of Michigan State University (YSI – MSU). After the study was conducted, its findings were reported to the Athletic Footwear Association in North Palm Beach, Florida. The Athletic Footwear Association, at the time, was composed of 88 manufacturers of athletic footwear and was part of the Sporting Goods Manufacturers Association.

Below is a summary of the study. First, it found that youth-age athletes fell into one of three broad categories: *reluctant, competent-oriented, or social players.* This finding is not surprising, as it conforms to the experience of most youth coaches. However, as the kids get older, the percentages in those categories begin to shift. That is, as the kids approach junior high and high school age, the percentage of reluctant players begins to drop significantly. Another study notes that by the age of 13, 75% of kids will have dropped out of youth sports. The top two reasons for quitting are not surprising: The activity is no longer fun, and they didn't care for the approach of the coach!

Based on my years of coaching experience, I can guarantee that YOU WILL HAVE some *reluctant players, some competent-oriented players, and some social players!* You will be required to prepare yourself for all three categories. Knowing this information up front and developing a teaching strategy to address each category of player will put you miles ahead as you enter your season, whether this is your first season of coaching or your 30th season of coaching. As you review the data below, focus on *what* the kids are telling us in this study.

Why kids play sports – three types of players

- **Reluctant players** – Kids whose involvement comes from peer or parental pressure. Make up about 25% of any team.

- **Competent-oriented players** – Practice and play hard to discover their abilities. Make up about 35% of any team.

- **Social players** – Drawn by external approval and rewards. Make up about 40% of any team.

By player type, the top 15 answers (from a total of 25 phrases) to the question:

"Why did you want to play your favorite school sport?"

Reluctant Player

1.	**Have fun**	**HAVE FUN**	**No. 1**
2.	Stay in shape		
3.	Get exercise		
4.	Improve skills		
5.	Do something I am good at		
6.	**Be part of a team**	**BE PART OF A TEAM**	**No. 6**
7.	Competitive excitement		
8.	Something to do		
9.	Be with friends		

10. Meet new friends
11. Team spirit
12. Learn new skills
13. **To win**   **TO WIN**   **No. 13**
14. Competitive challenge
15. Release tension

Social Player

1. Do something I am good at
2. **Have fun**   **HAVE FUN**   **No. 2**
3. Stay in shape
4. Competitive excitement
5. Improve skills
6. Reach higher levels
7. **Be part of a team**   **BE PART OF A TEAM**   **No. 7**
8. Get exercise
9. Competitive challenge
10. **To win**   **TO WIN**   **No. 10**
11. Learn new skills
12. Team spirit
13. Feel important
14. Trophies
15. Meet new friends

Competent-Oriented Player

1. Improve skills
2. Competitive excitement
3. Competitive challenge

4. Do something I am good at

5. **Have fun**   HAVE FUN   No. 5

6. **Be part of a team**   BE PART OF A TEAM   No. 6

7. Reach higher levels

8. **To win**   TO WIN   No. 8

9. Stay in shape

10. Learn new skills

11. Get exercise

12. Team spirit

13. Meet new friends

14. Like the coaches

15. Release tension

Analyze the MSU study when combining the three player types

Michigan State University Youth Sports Institute assigned numeric values to each response, and when the responses were analyzed, 10,000 children in 11 different cities were telling us the. **No. 1 reason** they play youth sports is to **have fun.**

The Overall Rankings When Combining the Three Groups:
(Reluctant Players, Social Players and Competent-Oriented Players)

1. **Have fun**   HAVE FUN   No. 1

2. Improve skills

3. Do something I am good at

4. Competitive excitement

5. Stay in shape

6. **Be part of a team**   BE PART OF A TEAM   No. 6

7. Get exercise

8. Competitive challenge

9. Reach higher level
10. **To win**   **TO WIN**   **No. 10**
11. Learn new skills
12. Meet new friends
13. Something to do
14. Be with friends
15. Feel important

As coaches, when preparing for practices and games, let's not forget what 10,000 children are telling us when asked: "Why did you want to play your favorite school sport?" It doesn't mean that winning isn't important; it just may not be as important as *we* think it should be for our players. No one coaches to lose. Challenge your players and be competitive, but at the same time, build fun into your practices and games and realize that as much as you may want to win, it clearly is not the *only* driving force as to why our children play a sport. Don't discount this survey because you may not agree with its findings. "Winning" almost didn't make the top 10 reasons as to why a child plays a school sport. We need to listen to our children. They are giving us the formula. If you do the first nine things on the above list well, you will achieve number 10, "to win."

Some observations about the study

- **Have fun** – Having fun ranked No. 1 and No. 2 for the Reluctant and the Social Player, respectively. Having fun ranked No. 5 for the Competent-Oriented Player. The kids have spoken. Work to make your coaching an enjoyable experience for everyone involved!

- **Be part of a team** – It almost cracked the top 5 (6th). I interpret this to mean, regardless of whether a child is a Reluctant player, a Competent-Oriented player, or a Social player, there is a high desire to belong to the team. We as coaches have a great influence over the acceptance of every child as an integral part of the team, regardless of a child's athletic ability or status among his or her friends.

- **To win** – 10,000 kids are telling us that winning isn't nearly as important as **we** think it is. Winning ranked 10th out of the 15 listed.

- **Learn new skills** – This came in 11th out of 15 listed. You may consider limiting your season objectives to allow the kids to "master" fewer skills, as opposed to exposing them to many skills and having them master none. Mastering skills builds confidence, gives the kids control, and makes for a more enjoyable experience.

  - Children want to master a skill.

  - They want control over that skill.

  - They want to feel good about attaining that skill.

  - They need successes.

  - Successes make them feel good.

  - Successes breed further successes.

Yelling vs. Teaching

Core Concept Number Three: The Concept of Yelling vs. Teaching:
Where do I begin with yelling vs. teaching? DON'T YELL!! Let me
make this very simple and direct: At the youth level, do not yell at
the kids, the officials, the parents, the administrators, or anyone
associated with a given sport or activity. One more time: If yelling is
part of your style, take it out of your teaching. If you want to yell, go
to the high school varsity level, the college level, or the professional
level. In fact, I have observed over the years that at all levels, yelling
has decreased significantly. Even at the higher levels of competition,
coaches are figuring out that old style approach of "kick butt and
take names" is simply not effective with today's athletes. Happily, we
are seeing less and less of this style in coaching.

There is a great story from one of Tony Dungy's books, *The Mentor
Leader,* with Nathan Whitaker. Tony, as a 14-year-old, went to a high
school basketball game with his dad. They watched one of the best
teams in the state of Michigan (River Rouge H.S.) that was coached
by a coaching legend, Lofton Greene, beat up on Tony's local high
school team. On the ride home, Tony's dad asked Tony about the
game. Tony answered with nothing but superlatives and compliments
about how well River Rouge played as a team on both offense
and defense. Then Tony's dad asked Tony about Coach Greene,
and Tony replied, "I wasn't very impressed with Coach Greene. He
didn't do anything. He just sat there calmly with his arms folded. No
expression. I didn't really see him do any coaching." Tony's dad then
replied, "When you're a teacher, you talk when you teach. You don't
talk during the test."

Coaches, I absolutely love that story. I will repeat what Tony's dad
said: *"When you're a teacher, you talk when you teach. You don't talk
during the test."* Coaches, the game is the test! How well have your
kids absorbed what you have been trying to teach them at practice?
Are they getting it? Did you see a great cutoff throw in baseball or
softball? Did you see a great outlet pass in hockey as your team
moved out of its end with the puck? Did you see a great pass from
your back-row player in volleyball to the setter? Did you see a great

screen in basketball? Did you see a great pass to space with your soccer team? Did you see a great pass route run in football?

The point is simple: You TEACH during practice, and you let the kids play the game with little or no yelling of instructions. This will allow the kids to make their own decisions. Are your kids learning the lessons of your practices? Are you allowing them to demonstrate their new knowledge, or are you constantly telling them what to do during a game?

Let them make mistakes. That is how a child learns. If you constantly yell instructions from the sidelines, you are NOT allowing your kids to make their own decisions, and more importantly, you are taking away their confidence in making their own decisions. They start to doubt their ability to make good choices. Let them fail, and when the time is right (on the bench during a game or at a practice), calmly explain what you wanted them to do and assure them that they can do just that.

This is a different approach to coaching for many of our coaches, but let me emphatically assure you that it works on so many levels. It is a teaching technique that has been used in classrooms forever. How many times during a test of any kind that you have taken (school or business) has a teacher or an instructor stood over you and yelled the correct answer to you? I am guessing that the answer is never! Therefore, during a game, why do we think we must lose our voice "coaching"?

Everyone knows you are the coach. You don't have to also be the play-by-play and analyst for every bounce of the basketball or every move in wrestling or every touch in volleyball or play in baseball or softball. Be their teacher, support their efforts, and calmly, in a nonthreatening manner, explain what you hoped had happened on a given play. Keep the focus on what you "wanted" to happen. Do not dwell on what the kid did wrong. If you dwell on the negative, that is what the child will remember.

Focus on what you "want" to happen in the future. And, finally, reassure them that you have great faith that they can successfully do whatever you have asked of them. That is teaching! Because it is a sport, we call it coaching, but it is effective teaching.

Yelling – What is so bad about it?

As an adult, how do you respond if someone was to yell at you? Even if you held your temper and responded as a centered adult, how did the yelling make you feel? Why do we think kids will respond any differently to yelling, whether the yelling is in anger or the constant yelling of sideline instructions?

Why shouldn't we yell at times?

- After all, the real world is tough, not always fun.
- Yelling gets results.
- Sometimes we protect our kids too much.
- A taste of the "real" world is not always a bad thing.

When do you think yelling is appropriate?

_____

_____

Is yelling ever appropriate?

_____

_____

Can there be "different" types of yelling? Explain.

_____

_____

Do you like to be yelled at?

OYes ONo

Yelling vs. Teaching

How can you tell if you have crossed the line?

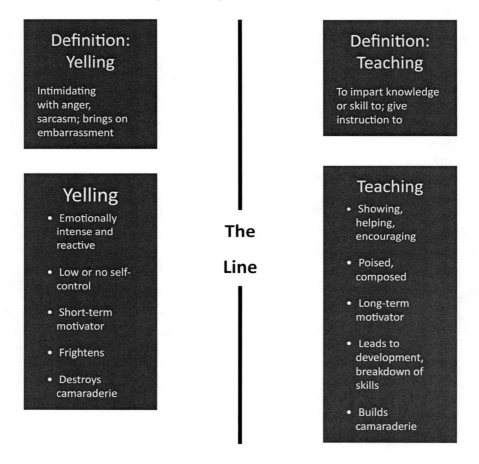

Definition: Yelling

Intimidating with anger, sarcasm; brings on embarrassment

Definition: Teaching

To impart knowledge or skill to; give instruction to

Yelling

- Emotionally intense and reactive
- Low or no self-control
- Short-term motivator
- Frightens
- Destroys camaraderie

The

Line

Teaching

- Showing, helping, encouraging
- Poised, composed
- Long-term motivator
- Leads to development, breakdown of skills
- Builds camaraderie

Raising Your Voice

Appropriate intensity and volume (example: alerting)
To the group: "I need your attention!"

How do kids view yelling vs. teaching?

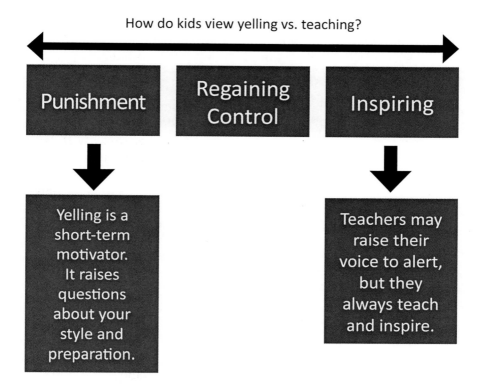

The louder we get, the less they learn.

Do you consider yourself a yeller or a teacher?

Coaching points

- **The more you are prepared, the more you will teach, and the more the kids will learn.**

- **The less you are prepared, the chances of yelling increase dramatically, and the likelihood of effectively teaching and learning decrease proportionately.**

- **Children and parents will always remember how you handled a child's mistake and the way in which you delivered the message. In addition, and regardless of the situation, children and parents will always remember how you made them feel.**

Core Concept Number Four: Self-Esteem Techniques:
Improving self-esteem requires two initiatives: 1) A supportive social environment (a supportive coach and team) and 2) Realistic goals (age-appropriate challenges).

The simple summary of instituting strong self-esteem techniques is; if a child does not feel good about himself/herself, typically they will quit a sport or given activity and you will not be able to teach them a new set of objectives in later years. Why? They won't be there.

Your on-field success will always be tied to how good your team is feeling about themselves and their ability to execute what you have been teaching at practice.

Self-Esteem Techniques

What do we call it when kids...

- Feel it's safe to learn (not flustered after making a mistake, not intimidated)

- Develop abilities (they achieve or grow as individuals)

- Feel like a part of the team (they fit in, belong)

It is called **self-esteem**: Kids learn to see themselves as capable and valued by others.

Children achieve a sense of self-worth when...

- They see themselves with abilities in areas that are important (scholastic, athletic, social, behavioral, physical appearance).

- They see themselves as valued and socially accepted by others.

Improving self-esteem takes two things

1. A supportive social environment (a supportive coach and team)
2. Realistic goals (age-appropriate challenges)

Chapter 3

Coaching Philosophy, Goals, and Expectations

Coaching Coaches Pyramid – Philosophy, Goals, and Expectations

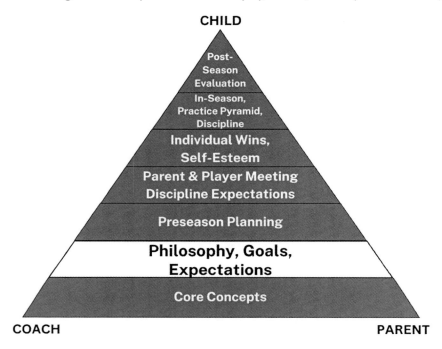

CHILD

Post-Season Evaluation

In-Season, Practice Pyramid, Discipline

Individual Wins, Self-Esteem

Parent & Player Meeting Discipline Expectations

Preseason Planning

Philosophy, Goals, Expectations

Core Concepts

COACH   **PARENT**

As we move up the Coaching Pyramid to consider Philosophy, Goals, and Expectations, you might be asking yourself, "Did I really sign up for all this? We haven't touched the field or the court or the mats or the ice, and I am already overwhelmed!" I get it. I have been here many times before. Let me assure you that every second you put into your pyramid, or your process preparation, will come back to you a hundredfold during your season. Plus, once you get your basic program in place, you will only tweak it over the next several years. The hardest part is in year one when you are establishing your own pyramid and your own processes. Hang in there. I have given you the map. Your job is to do the driving and listening to that recorded voice when she says, "Turn left in 500 feet." That is your individual responsibility as you prepare for the upcoming season.

Effective Philosophy, Goals, and Expectations become the foundation of your program for YOU, your assistant coaches, your players, and your parents. This one section will determine whether your program is inferior, OK, or great. My guess is, we all want a *great* program. If so, then do the work! Your up-front work makes all the difference! Remember, nothing you do today is written in concrete. Anything can be adjusted at any time if need be. YOU are the coach, and this is your program, your process. I suspect that you can sit down at your computer and within an hour or two, you can develop your own Philosophy, Goals, and Expectations for yourself, your assistant coaches, your players, and your parents. You don't have to write a book. Keep it simple. Keep it direct. Also, don't panic at this request. I will show you more detail in Chapter 5 when we talk about the parent/player meeting. Your Philosophy, Goals, and Expectations are highlighted during that meeting.

Refer to the following pages to see a snapshot of details for developing your Philosophy, Goals, and Expectations.

Developing your coaching style starts with...

1. Your Coaching Philosophy
2. Your Coaching Goals
3. Your Coaching Expectations

Coaching Philosophy

Prior to developing your coaching philosophy, seek out your organization's mission statement along with your sport's or activity's mission statement.

Based on what we have discussed thus far, what is your coaching philosophy? Your coaching philosophy is your mission. Some reminders on developing your coaching philosophy:

- The fun factor: Where does winning fit in?
- Coaching as a teacher/an educator
- Coaching as a form of giving back
- Kids say they want to be a part of a team
- Yelling vs. teaching: Be a positive ambassador for your community
- What do you want your team to look like?
- **Where does your character fit into your program?**

Finally, outside of the Xs and Os, skills and drills, and the strategies of the game, how is your program defined?

As a coach of children, my coaching philosophy is:

_____

_____

_____

_____

_____

_____

_____

_____

_____

_____

_____

_____

_____

_____

Coaching Goals

As a reminder, make your goals:

- Age-appropriate

- Reasonable and, if possible, measurable

- What age-appropriate goals do you really want to accomplish this season?

- What 3, 4, 5, or 12 goals are attainable with your team?

- Do your goals tie into a two-, three-, or four-year plan? (assuming you will keep these kids for some time)

As a coach of children, **my specific sport-related coaching goals** for this season are:

_____

_____

_____

_____

_____

_____

_____

_____

Coaching Expectations

Making your philosophy and goals real means coaches need to set the proper tone from the beginning. This means **stating your expectations** in three basic areas:

- How can parents expect you to treat their children?
- How do you expect parents and children to treat you?
- How do you expect children, parents, and coaches to behave?

See Chapter 5: Parent/Player Meeting for more details on setting and delivering expectations.

As a coach of children, my expectations for this season are:

_____

_____

_____

_____

_____

_____

_____

The above are simple exercises that you can adjust at any time. However, it gives a piece of the puzzle as you begin to build your program and your processes. Thanks again for coaching our kids!

Chapter 4

Preseason Planning

Coaching Coaches Pyramid – Preseason Planning

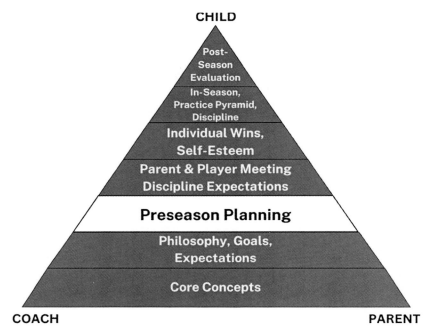

CHILD

Post-Season Evaluation

In-Season, Practice Pyramid, Discipline

Individual Wins, Self-Esteem

Parent & Player Meeting Discipline Expectations

Preseason Planning

Philosophy, Goals, Expectations

Core Concepts

COACH   **PARENT**

PRESEASON PLANNING: Congratulations on your move up the Coaching Pyramid! You have built a strong base for your program by reflecting on and integrating your Core Concepts. Well done!

In addition, you have bolstered your pyramid by developing your Philosophy, Goals, and Expectations. You are well on your way to delivering a highly effective and positive sporting program! Good for you! Great start!

So, what do you do with these building blocks? How do you start to put your hard work of building your pyramid into a real application for your players and parents? The next step in your program is Preseason Planning. What does that checklist look like? The list presented later in the chapter is designed to get you started and let you see what a Preseason Planning checklist looks like. I encourage you to add or subtract anything from the list to meet your specific needs and those of your players. YOU are the coach!

In the worksheet that follows, I ask you to list what you think should be included in a Preseason Planning list. Take a shot on your own at listing some action items. You may hit upon something that I did not think of that may be important to your own program. For example, you might have some kids with special needs, or you may be coaching in a league that is devoted exclusively to kids with special needs. Not every coach has the exact set of circumstances.

However, the principles of setting up a program remain the same. Regardless of why you are coaching children, your first responsibility to your players and their families is YOUR ability to be organized and transparent with your program. I am convinced that you are well on your way to delivering a highly effective program for your team and your parents. Remember, coaching always come down to WHO you are (your character) and HOW you deliver your program! Thanks for coaching our kids!

Preseason Planning

Preseason Planning starts the process of building the foundation for a successful and enjoyable season for everyone involved (kids, parents, and coach). Your ability to properly prepare for the season will deliver a powerful message to both the parents and kids about your program, your organizational skills, and your willingness to provide the best experience possible.

List action items you think coaches should do as part of the preseason activities:

_____

_____

_____

_____

_____

_____

_____

_____

_____

_____

_____

Preseason Checklist

The preseason checklist is designed to help a coach effectively prepare for the upcoming season and give thought to specific areas of preseason planning. Specific items to consider:

1. Begin to develop your personal coaching philosophy, goals, and expectations.

2. Start your coach's binder (1½" or 2" three-ring binder).

3. Get your team roster, player registration forms, rule books, organization's constitution, and coaches' handbook.

4. Know the contact to go to, within your organization, for questions.

5. Review the player registration forms.

6. Call each family. Make it a positive first contact (What question do you want to ask every year? Coach to the Parent: "Are there any medical issues that we as a coaching staff need to be aware of regarding your child?" If yes, take copious notes and stay in close contact with those parents. Just asking the question tells the parents that you have your act together and your number one concern is their child.)

7. Draft an introductory letter/email to the kids and parents. Obviously, you can send an email and/or text with your introductory letter, but I've found that sending an actual letter directly to the kids and parents was an even bigger deal. Imagine receiving a letter from your coach or teacher; that is a big deal. (It is worthy of being posted on the refrigerator!)

8. Develop an Items to Know sheet that includes any specific organization requirements.

9. Develop a roster of the kids and include the parents' first names and phone numbers.
   Get permission for cell phone numbers/home numbers and how to enter family information if you are dealing with a two-household scenario. Make sure to get parental approval for contact information and distribution to other team members' families.

10. Send your first letter (or email or text) introducing your philosophy and inviting them to your parent/player meeting. This meeting could be before or after your first or second practice—the earlier the better, but before your first practice is always the best!

11. I realize that social media presents many other possibilities to communicate with the families. Use what works best for you and your families.

12. Start to prepare for your parent/player meeting.

    a. Philosophy, goals, and expectations (previously described in Chapter 3)

    b. The Code of Excellence (Chapter 5)

    c. Parent Participation Agreement (Chapter 5)

    d. Items to Know sheet for the families (Chapter 4)

    e. Roster with the parents' names (Chapter 4)

    f. Schedules (if available) and maps to the fields/gyms/rinks (Chapter 4)
    (Again, I realize that with Google Maps or other map apps, you typically don't need hard copy maps, but some fields do not have official addresses, and it may be difficult to find them. Again, do what works best for you and your families.)

    g. Anything else that you can think of to discuss that will help everyone involved strive for a positive experience

13. As coaches, review the rule book.

14. Check the condition of all your equipment and encourage the kids to do the same with their equipment.

15. Provide for first aid:

    a. Ice at all practices and games

    b. First aid kit for all practices and games

    c. Encourage coaches to attend classes. Seek out specific components/modules/information on:

        - **First aid**

        - **CPR**

        - **AED**

        - **Concussions**

16. Develop an injury plan of action.

Children with Medical Conditions

Make sure you educate yourself on medical conditions that may affect children on your roster. Ask the parents if there are any medical issues that you need to know about. For multiple hours a week, over an extended period, you are with children who potentially represent a variety of medical conditions. You are no different than a teacher in a classroom. For you to be on top of your game, you need to know as much as you can about each child, assuming the parents are willing to share information about their child's medical history or any disability with you, as their child's coach.

If a family shares that information with you, take some time to educate yourself about the condition(s) and prepare effective response plans. Here are some common child-related medical conditions:

> **ADD/ADHD** (Attention Deficit Disorder or Attention Deficit Hyperactivity Disorder) – Children with ADD/ADHD may have attention issues (focus) and potential discipline issues (hyperactivity). Be sure to seek additional advice from the parents.
>
> **Asthma** – A difficult breathing condition that can compromise a child and his or her athletic performance. Seek additional advice from the parents.
>
> **Autism** – A disorder of neural development. It can affect communication and social interaction. There are varying degrees of autism. The parents can provide the best methods for dealing with their child. In some cases, you may want the parent to assist during all practices and games.
>
> **Allergies** – Can range from very mild to quite severe. In some cases, it can seriously impact performance. Most people think of outdoor allergens. However, some allergies may be food-related. A peanut allergy, as well as other food allergies, can be very dangerous for children. Once again, the best source of information about a specific child is his or her parents. Is an Epi-pen required at all practices and games?

Obesity – Unfortunately, many children today are obese or close to it. We recommend that you do **not** push an overweight child or generally out-of-shape child to prove a point. Consult with the parents as to the best way to work with their overweight or out-of-shape child. Encourage the parents to get advice from their family doctor about their child's weight as it may impact their ability to participate.

Coaches (head coaches and assistant coaches), be on top of your game. As best you can, know the kids, their general health, absorb any input from their parents, and prepare accordingly. Your ability to consult with each parent about each child will help you develop the safest environment for everyone associated with your program.

Also, be sure to consult with your assistant coaches and make sure they share with you any health conditions that affect them. In turn, share any health conditions that may affect you.

Remember, you are building a program!

Sample Letters to Parents

This letter represents a generic introduction from the coach to the parents.

Introduction letter

Current Date

Dear *Child Name* and Parents:

My name is *Head Coach Name*, and I will be coaching your *List Activity* team this year. I am very excited about the opportunity to work with each of you. My coaching philosophy is quite simple. First and foremost, I want each child to feel good about himself/herself. A strong self-esteem is vital to learning. Second, I want the kids to have fun!! Third, I want the kids to learn some *List Activity* concepts and improve on their individual skills.

My definition of winning might be different than most. I believe that "wins" come in various sizes and shapes, just like the kids themselves. A good throw-in in soccer, a good screen in basketball, a good set in volleyball, a good cutoff throw in baseball/softball, or a good pass of the baton in track are all considered "wins" in my book. My job as a coach, and I believe your job as a parent/supporter, is to recognize these various "wins" and provide the necessary feedback that reinforces the behavior that makes these "wins" possible. If we, as parents/coaches, focus on the individual "wins," the scoreboard will take care of itself.

As a parent, your willingness to have your child participate is a big commitment on your part, and I sincerely appreciate your efforts. Also, if there are any parents who wish to coach, please contact me. I welcome all help. Please get involved. I may be calling you!

Enclosed you will find:
- An Items to Know sheet
- A roster with parent names
- A schedule and maps to the fields or addresses for all the fields

I also wish to host a Parent/Player Meeting for about 20 minutes *before/after* our first practice, which is scheduled for *Practice Date, Time, and Location*. Please have at least one parent attend this meeting.

Thanks for allowing *Child Name* to play this season. If any of the above prompts any questions or needs clarification, please contact me via the phone numbers or email address below.

Let's enjoy this season together!

Coach Name
Primary Coach Phone Number/Alternate Coach Phone Number
Coach Email Address/Alternate Coach Email Address

Advanced Letter

This letter represents introduction communication from the coach to the parents when the coach has worked with the families for several years.

Current Date

Girls Softball is Back!!!

Issue 1-1, Coach *Last Name* Press

City, State – The 5th Grade Girls coached by Coach *Last Name* and a host of parents is back and getting ready for the season! With an active off-season, the prospect of playing on dirt infields (as opposed to all-grass fields), the addition of new equipment bags to haul the "stuff" around, and a couple of new softballs, the team begins its rigorous spring training schedule. With the thought that this year's team may even play on dirt infields, the training takes an early tough turn by practicing on the school's asphalt!! When asked about this strategy, Coach *Last Name* said, "If it's not green, we are practicing on it!"

Similar thoughts were conveyed by *Assistant Coach 1, Assistant Coach 2, Assistant Coach 3, and Assistant Coach 4*: "Bring on the asphalt, and don't forget the chalk; we need bases, you know." Also, reflecting on the year was *Child Name 1, Child Name 2, Child Name 3, and Child Name 4*, jointly saying: "We are in the 5th grade. Our time has come." When asked about their statement, the players weren't sure what it meant but said it sounded good.

And finally, from *Child Name 1, Child Name 2, and Child Name 3* comes the following: "It doesn't matter who they throw at us. Bring on your 'heater.' We're still going to 'beat her'."

Obviously, the enthusiasm is running high as the impending season grows near. Coach *Last Name* has a host of volunteers and says that any parent is welcome to participate at any time. Also, relayed to this reporter was Coach *Last Name's* basic philosophy:

- Let's promote strong self-esteem, both on the field and at home.
- Let's enjoy this experience with our kids; let's have fun with these *10- and 11-year-olds.*
- Let's learn some softball and make every effort to better ourselves as players, coaches, and parents.
- And finally, let us, the coaches and parents, provide the example of good sportsmanship.

This season has all the makings of an exciting year. Coach *Last Name* hopes that the players and their parents enjoy this season. If at any time, you need to contact Coach *Last Name*, do so via the information below.

Note: The following page shows our practices for the month of *Month Name* and batting cage times for the first month. Also included is an Items to Know sheet, a roster, a schedule, and maps to the fields.

Thanks for being such good families. It is an honor to coach your kids.

Coach Name
Primary Coach Phone Number/Email Address
Alternate Coach Phone Number/Email Address

Items to Know

The Items to Know sheet allows you to share and set some basic expectations for the families. Key sections within the Items to Know sheet are:

Schedule (practice and game)

1. Practice Schedule – We practice *Dates and Start/End Times* at *Location*.

2. Games – Games will be played at *Locations* (Check schedules for game time and be there on time.)

3. Rainouts – You will receive a call from me or another parent between 5:15 & 5:30 p.m. No need to call me—**just show up unless you hear from me or another parent**. (You may want to add an email address or text number here or inform them about a group email or text procedure for rainouts, changes, etc.)

Equipment

- All kids need *List Equipment.*
- List shoe rules (for example, *plastic spikes, no metal spikes*)
- Bring water to all practices and games.
- Our uniform consists of *List Uniform Shirt Color, Pants Color, Socks Color, etc.*
- Our team's uniform coordinator is *Uniform Coordinator Name.*

Rules and policies

- As coach, I am responsible for the fans' behavior. Your cooperation is appreciated.
- Please review the Code of Excellence and the Parent Participation Agreement.

Volunteers

We need a postgame goodies coordinator to provide drinks or a snack after each game. There is no need to spend much money on this. Just provide enough to cover the players and any small siblings. I will ask parents about possible food allergies.

Miscellaneous announcements (if required)

Please bring a check for $ *amount* made out to *Organization Name* as a uniform deposit.

Team Roster Format

Coaches, today most team rosters are included on team apps. If you choose to include a team roster in your handouts, please keep the information to an absolute minimum. I always included a team roster so that parents could learn each other's names and get to know each other better by using first names. In my program/process, that was the only reason for a team roster.

Header Information

> Title — Team Roster
>
> Activity — specific sport or activity
>
> Grade
>
> Year

Head Coach Information

> Head coach name
>
> Head coach primary phone number
>
> Head coach email address

Assistant Coach Information

> Assistant coach name
>
> Assistant coach primary phone number
>
> Assistant coach email address

Child Information

> Uniform number
>
> Child's first name only

Parent Information

>Parents' first names only

Team Schedule Format

Coaches, a team schedule should include the following information:

Header Information

>Title – Team Schedule

>Activity– Specific sport or activity

>Grade

>Year

Head Coach Information

>Head coach name

>Head coach primary phone number

>Head coach email address

Assistant Coach Information

>Assistant coach name

>Assistant coach primary phone number

>Assistant coach email address

Activity Information

      Day of week

      Activity date

      Opponent

      Address

      Location

      Start time

      ** BE THERE TIME (BTT)

      Practice/Game

**I used this technique to grab everyone's attention. I used to tell the kids and parents that if a game started at 2:00 pm, I wanted the kids there by 1:38 pm. I found that the kids and parents paid more attention if I used a one-off time by the minute. We had fun with it and it prompted the parents to get their kids to the games on time. In fact, the kids always knew the BTT and would, without me being present, put pressure on their parents to get them to the game on time. *The kids spoke for me.* "Mom and dad, we have to go. I need to be there by 1:38. Let's go!!" We had fun with this technique and I got a lot funny comments from the parents, but the bottom line was, the kids got to the games on time!!

Maps

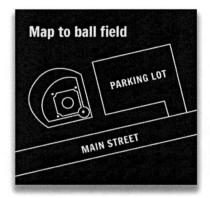
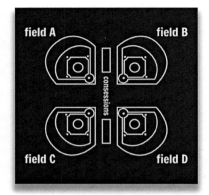

Most gymnasiums have a specific street address and ZIP code. Assuming parents are given this information from you, they can easily look up directions or use a map app.

Frequently used playing fields are known by most families, and they will know how to get there without the use of a map.

However, some fields are difficult for anyone to find easily and will not have a specific street address. Help the families by providing maps of out-of-the-way fields. It will be appreciated and save you time in the long run. It is a small thing, but it is yet another way to help build an effective program.

Chapter 5

Parent/Player Meeting

Coaching Coaches Pyramid – Parent/Player Meeting

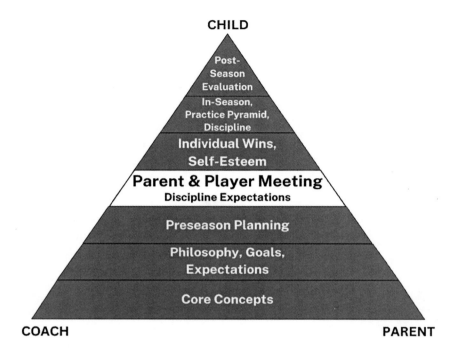

CHILD

Post-Season Evaluation

In-Season, Practice Pyramid, Discipline

Individual Wins, Self-Esteem

Parent & Player Meeting
Discipline Expectations

Preseason Planning

Philosophy, Goals, Expectations

Core Concepts

COACH   **PARENT**

Parent/Player Meeting (Discipline Expectations): You have now spent a good deal of time understanding your Core Concepts, establishing your Philosophy, Goals, and Expectations, and you have put a good deal of time into your Preseason Planning. But guess what? You haven't even stepped onto the field of play yet. That is absolutely fine! That is the way it should be. You are building toward the season by establishing yourself and your program as the place to be. I want you to win over your players and your parents (families) before you blow one whistle. Coaching (teaching) goes way beyond the Xs and Os. Families must have confidence in you and your program. What are you about? What drives you as a coach? As a family, why should I be thrilled that you are our coach? You are about to deliver the answers to the above questions.

During the parent/player meeting, you have a unique opportunity to establish yourself, your coaches, and your program as the place to be for the next 90 to 120 days. If your meeting is delivered effectively and respectfully, parents and kids will beat a path to your program and brag about having YOU as their coach. I can almost guarantee it. Why? Because most coaches do not establish themselves and their program on the front end with a well-organized meeting to set up the season. Be advised, however: It is not good enough to just enumerate the "dos and don'ts" of the season during this meeting. You must effectively *sell* yourself and your program! Remember, coaching always comes down to WHO you are and HOW you deliver your program. If you go through all the work of effectively preparing for this meeting and then deliver it as a boot camp drill sergeant, you will have set yourself and your program back to a point that may not be retrievable.

I am very serious about your delivery. Your delivery of you and your program must be straightforward and friendly! Presenting yourself in this way will not only relieve any anxiety your players and parents have, it will also allow you to pave the way for them to better understand and agree to your expectations. If you deliver your program as an authoritarian drill sergeant or pompous know-it-all, the parents will spend their entire drive home questioning what they have done. Instead, you want them leaving your meeting saying to their kids on the ride home, "This is so great! You're in a great situation with a great coach and coaching staff. This is going to be fun!"

Beyond merely delivering the expectations of your program, you want every child and parent leaving your meeting so pumped up that they cannot wait for the first practice to begin! As the maxim goes, "You only get one opportunity to make a good first impression." Along with your first call to the kids and parents welcoming them, this meeting is a close second for making a "first" good impression! Be courteous to a fault, be direct and matter-of-fact with your expectations, smile a lot, and embrace the moment. This is truly your first classroom every year. You are in complete control. You are highly organized. *You are appropriately friendly*. You are confident in every one of your expectations.

Finally, here is the untold secret about the parent/player meeting: If you don't have some bizarre expectation (for example: prohibiting parents from attending practices or games), the kids and parents will buy into your program in a big way because **they are NOT in the heat of the battle**. The season has not even started. *If your expectations are reasonable*, sharing them *before* the season has begun will result in a much higher acceptance of you and your program. It makes all the difference to establish reasonable expectations before you ever step onto the field of play.

A second benefit of a preseason parent/player meeting is that it forces you to prepare. It forces you to establish your comprehensive expectations. It forces you to meet all the parents and kids before the first practice. You get to effectively *sell* your program in a public forum. **Assistant coaches are not exempt from your expectations.** It is highly important that both the kids and the parents understand this point. All your stakeholders in this endeavor (remember the three points of the Coaching Pyramid: children, coaches, and parents) are being held to a high standard. Everyone! When it is all said and done, this is the most important meeting/practice of your season. **Make it a good one!**

Finally, with the kids present, discuss your 7 Steps to Discipline (presented later in the chapter). Since the kids are present, you should weigh your words wisely and present this section age appropriately. However, go over the steps so that *everyone* understands your approach to any discipline issues. I will guarantee you that setting these discipline expectations *up front* will serve you well as you move through your season.

SIDE NOTE: I have great confidence that you will have little or no discipline issues if you run your practices as I outline later in the book. By doing so, the kids will not have time to "step out of line," and before you know it, the practice will be over. However, it is still critically important that you address this issue of discipline with everyone in the room. Be sure you deliver the message as the caring person you are who understands that kids, at times, will be kids and misstep when it comes to behavior. My hope is that discipline will be a small issue for all of you, but if you have a behavior issue, you will have already established the guidelines and action items that you will take to correct the situation.

Again, a parent will be far less likely to take issue with your response to a discipline problem if you follow your own guidelines that were discussed during the parent/player meeting. You are out ahead of this potential issue because you made it an expectation before you ever had a practice. That's one of the beauties of the parent/ player meeting. If you follow your own expectations, especially when it comes to discipline, you are in a good place if you are ever challenged.

When it comes to discipline issues, be friendly, be empathetic, be consistent, and be willing to work with the child and their parents if they reach out to you for an explanation or solicit your help in correcting the player's behavior. If challenged, try to establish an alliance with the parents to help everyone involved reach a successful solution for the child. The child is the focus—not the parents and not the coaches. (Please understand, the discipline issues I am referring to deal with a child misbehaving with their teammates or possibly disrespecting a coach, official, or another adult.)

NOT to be discussed in your parent/player meeting: If you ever encounter a situation where a child accuses a coach or another parent or anyone else with any kind of abuse (verbal or otherwise), get your organization involved immediately! The chance of such an accusation is quite small, but as the head coach, you need to be prepared to escalate an accusation of that kind and let the organization deal with the family. You may or may not be asked to participate further if an investigation ensues, but this is clearly far beyond what you initially signed up for. Again, the chances of something like this happening are very low, but simply be aware that it is a possibility. Anyone managing people of any age needs to, at least, give some thought to this possibility and how they will respond.

The next several pages will give you a step-by-step outline of a parent/player meeting. Use any part of it that works well for you, your coaches, your parents, and players.

This part of the pyramid may be the most important building block. Address it with a good attitude and it will become a game changer when it comes to establishing your program. Remember, coaching always comes down to WHO you are and HOW you deliver your program! Thanks again for coaching.

Parent/Player Meeting

It is highly recommended that every coach prepares for and conducts a parent/player meeting prior to the start of every season. The agenda below will assist in developing an effective meeting for both parents and kids.

Parent/Player Meeting **AGENDA**

Introductions

- Head coach and assistant coaches
- Qualifications and background
- Talk about why you went into coaching

Coaching philosophy, goals, and expectations

- Coaching philosophy – share your coaching philosophy
- The role of winning and having fun
- Code of Excellence
- Parent Participation Agreement

Program specifics

- Items to know
- Roster
- Schedules
- Maps
- Questions and answers
- Postseason Evaluation – available for all families

Fan behavior

- Sideline behavior – before, during, and after the games and practices
- Parents, grandparents, siblings, other family members, and friends a family member may bring
- As the head coach, you are responsible for everyone's behavior

Other organizational announcements

- Organizational expectations, e.g., uniform deposits, concession stand work hours

Code of Excellence Introduction

The objective of the Code of Excellence is to share with the parents and kids the standards by which this program (team) is going to operate. These standards directly affect the coach, the parents, and the kids. By using this document, a coach can quickly and easily share foundational expectations for everyone.

The key to this document is the inclusion of the coach. The coach is not sitting in an ivory tower simply dictating what everyone else should be doing. This document holds all three groups (coach, parents, and child) accountable to a set of standards.

The Code of Excellence is a two-sided, single-page document. The front side of the document lists the responsibilities of the coach, parents, and child. The front side can be populated in any way to fit the needs of the coach's program. The back side of the document contains room for parent and child notes, as well as the parent policies. In the parent and child notes sections, a parent and/or child can share any additional information that they may not have wanted to share at a public meeting or even face-to-face with the coach.

The more information a coach can gather about a family and child, the more prepared he or she will be to provide the best possible sporting experience for everyone involved.

At the parent/player meeting, each family will receive two copies of the Code of Excellence. The parent(s) will take both copies home and discuss the code with the child. One copy will be signed by the child and parent(s) and returned to the coach. The second copy will be kept by the family for future reference and family discussion.

Coach, take this form seriously. It will not only help you set specific expectations, it will also help define your program for the kids, the families, your coaching staff, your organization, and yourself.

Code of Excellence

Code of excellence front side

	Sportsmanship	Respect	Responsibility
Coach	• Recognize and encourage efforts regardless of results. • Provide opportunities for all athletes regardless of ability. • Promote vigorous competition while treating opponents as "friends at play."	• Acknowledge and respect anyone associated with the program (model the Golden Rule). • Model dignity, poise, and composure in dealings with parents, kids, coaches, and officials. • Promote harmonious relationships through a desire to understand respectful communication.	• Provide a safe, fun environment that promotes growth and self-esteem. • Communicate with parents, kids, and officials in a timely manner. • Know the rules and policies of the sport. • Meet and maintain appropriate standards of coaching excellence.
Parent	• Provide positive encouragement at games and practices. • Model sportsmanlike conduct toward other parents, spectators, kids, coaches, and officials.	• Model respect for authority both on and off the field, especially during practices and games. • Make good-faith efforts to honor timely participation in games and at practices.	• Adhere to rules, regulations, policies, and procedures of governing organizations, especially the Parent Participation Agreement. • Support and participate in appropriate discipline of your child. • Proactively help in whatever way you can, e.g., being on time for the start and end of practices and games.
Youth	• Have fun. • Play hard. • Play fair.	• Follow the Golden Rule. • Show respect for parents, coaches, teammates, officials, and especially opponents.	• Show up at all practices and games (on time), unless the coach has been notified. • Cooperate.

_____   _____   _____   _____
Coach   Date   Parent   Date

_____   _____   _____   _____
Youth   Date   Parent   Date

Code of Excellence back side

Code of Excellence parent policies

- If you speak from the sidelines, it must be positive.
- No coaching from the sidelines.
- Make practices and games "quality time" for your families.
- Create "quality time" for you and your child.

Questions, comments, and concerns for the coach

Parents, please use this section to share any additional information that you deem necessary with the coach.

Parent Notes:

_____

_____

_____

_____

Youth Notes:

_____

_____

_____

_____

Parent Participation Agreement

The Parent Participation Agreement is designed to help promote effective communication between the coach and the families. Here are some examples and guidelines for two different forms of communication.

How to communicate with the coach

Parents, please use this as a guideline when you need to communicate with your coach.

Informational or simple communication examples

- We are going on vacation...

- Jill had a 102° fever today...

- We will be late next week because...

  Coaches welcome this form of communication early and often. The more parents communicate with coaches, the better.

  However, if the communication is sensitive in nature or possibly emotional, please follow the guidelines below.

Sensitive or emotional communication guidelines

- Exercise good judgment and restraint when offering input that may be considered critical or sensitive in nature. In other words, **think about it** (coach will do the same).

- If you feel it is necessary to offer your input, **please wait 24 hours** after the game, practice, or event that triggered your concern.

- All potentially critical or sensitive communications **must take place** at a time and location other than during practice, at a game, on the parking lot, in front of other people, or in front of one's own child or another child.

Discipline

Parents have the primary responsibility for disciplining their children. The program has a three-step process in dealing with children who need corrective input about their behavior.

1. The coach will give a simple warning that focuses on the child's behavior.

2. The coach may give the child a second warning before a time-out or go straight to a brief time-out.

3. If the behavior persists, you (the parent) will be contacted and asked to participate in appropriate steps to correct your child's behavior.

7 Steps to Discipline

1. The more you are organized in all phases of your coaching, the fewer problems you will have.

2. Develop a philosophy of behavior that you expect, then communicate it clearly and often to both the players and their parents.

3. Prepare yourself to handle discipline problems in a low-key manner and institute a matter-of-fact approach. Remember, most discipline problems are the result of a child not getting enough attention either from you or his or her peers.

4. Once a low-key warning has been given to a specific child or group of children and the child or group continues to act up, a simple time-out away from all the other kids is appropriate (approximately 5 minutes). **Make sure to keep the child or children within your sight if this action is taken.**

- It can also be very effective to address the inappropriate behavior in a one-on-one setting, with another coach in attendance so you are not considered "alone" with the child.

5. If a specific child (or group of children) demonstrates an ongoing discipline problem, and you have attempted to discipline the child with time-outs, you have talked to the child one-on-one, and you still see no improvement, get the parents involved **immediately**. Solicit the parents' help and form an alliance with the parents to resolve the issue.

6. If you do not get the appropriate support from the parents, you may have no choice but to seek the director of your sport and/or the board of your organization for help. You cannot be an effective coach if you are constantly battling discipline problems. **It just won't work!**

7. Remember steps No. 1 and No. 2: The more you are organized in all phases of your coaching, the fewer problems you will have. Develop a philosophy of behavior that you expect, then communicate it clearly and often to both the players and their parents.

*   A final thought: Work hard to avoid sarcasm. The younger players don't understand your "shot," and the older players become embarrassed and will build walls that may never come down.

Chapter 6

Individual Wins

Coaching Coaches Pyramid – Individual Wins and Self-Esteem

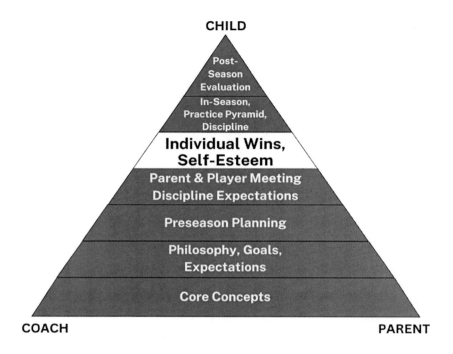

Individual Wins/Self-Esteem: Coaches, now you are on your field of play, practices have begun, and games are within a few weeks of starting. You are out there doing your thing! You are actually coaching (teaching). You may be entering this season with years of experience or you may be stepping onto your field of play for the first time as a coach. Either way, THANK YOU for coaching our kids! As mentioned before, the impact (positively or negatively) that you have on these kids and parents will last a lifetime. Think about that sobering sentence for a second. What you do today as a coach will be remembered by these kids and their parents for the rest of their lives. How do you want to be remembered? Do you what to be that uncompromising coach who demands respect rather than working to earn it? I can assure you that a demanding coaching style is easier to implement than an effective teacher style. A demanding coaching style is typically an "in-your-face" style. It is aggressive.

Is that style necessary with this age group? The answer is no. An effective teaching style is certainly harder, but in the long run, it is so much more effective. Remember, you may have many of these kids for years. What I am asking of you as a youth coach is a long-term commitment.

About 30 years ago, coaches noticed that kids and parents started to question that aggressive approach. As a society, we began to more carefully question authority figures. Though thoughtful individuals were not necessarily trying to be mean-spirited, they nevertheless wanted to know why they were being asked or required to do something a certain way.

This more critical questioning occurred in many areas with structures and individuals who held a traditional leadership role; doctors, police officers, politicians, employers, teachers, and many others came under increased scrutiny. People did not simply accept an authority figure because of the diploma hanging on the wall or the whistle around their neck. They wanted to know why something was being required of them.

In addition, as a society, we began to recognize that demeaning someone to achieve an end goal was counterproductive. That realization slowly made its way into the world of sports, and that was a good thing. Consequently, the "kick butt and take names" style of coaching started to fall by the wayside, and a much more cooperative, inclusive, and empathetic form of coaching began to emerge. Unfortunately, we still have coaches who are coaching our young kids who want to emulate that aggressive approach and who believe that screaming and yelling is coaching. Let me assure you that this style is "old school" and is on its way out.

Admittedly, it is so much harder to coach as a teacher. It takes more time, it takes more convincing, it takes more preparation, and it takes more buy-in. It is so much easier to scream at kids and demand that they do something one way (and, of course, that is the coach's way).

I told you early on that teaching is difficult and to be a great teacher is especially difficult. That is such a true statement. Remember, everything you do on that field of play is creating memories for a lifetime. I believe we owe it to our kids to be the BEST WE CAN BE. Yelling and screaming must not be a part of your playbook in youth sports. If you think or know that you are a screamer and yeller, look hard in the mirror right now and vow to yourself that you will change your approach to coaching. It will not be easy, but I guarantee you that you will create relationships with these kids and families that you never thought possible. In addition, assuming you have a child on your team, the gift you will be giving your child will also last a lifetime. I have been a part of coaching where yelling was very much the norm, and I have been a part of coaching where teaching was the norm, and I can confidently state that the teaching approach was so much more rewarding. It not only helped create better players, it also helped produce more confident players, better people, and far better memories for everyone involved. Was it harder? ABSOLUTELY! Was it more rewarding? ABSOLUTELY!

Another Story: Years ago, as a rookie high school football coach in Ohio, I assigned a rarely used sophomore a spot on the kicking team as a reward for working particularly hard in practice. On game day, it was clear that this young player was very nervous to see live varsity action. His assigned spot was just to the right of the kicker.

Our squad received the kickoff to begin the game, so John didn't get in on that play. But near the end of the half, our team scored, and with seven seconds to play, we had to kick off to our opponents. John went out for the kickoff, and, probably due to nerves, took his place on the wrong side of the kicker!

Though I noticed the problem from the press box, I couldn't fix the issue prior to the kickoff. And, predictably, the receiving team returned the kick for a touchdown right up the lane where John was supposed to be. I was livid with his mistake, and I made a beeline to the locker room to confront him. Once in the locker room, I pulled him aside and proceeded to scream (and I mean, scream!) at this kid for 15 to 20 seconds because he lined up on the wrong side of the kicker and the other team used that gap to return the kickoff for a touchdown. It got to the point that other coaches said to me, "Bill, that is enough. We have other adjustments that need to be made at halftime." But the damage was done. John was worthless for the rest of the game. We had to take him off the kickoff team. I had not only rendered him useless to the team, I had completely broken this kid.

Shame on me! I felt very bad about screaming at John. I felt bad after the game. I felt bad all day Saturday. I felt bad all day Sunday. No one deserves to be treated like that—no one!

On Monday morning, I pulled John out of his first-period class to express three thoughts: 1) I am so sorry for how I screamed at you on Friday night. That was not me coaching. That was me being mad and venting. I was wrong in how I treated you. Please accept my apology. 2) I am going to apologize to the team at practice today. 3) I vowed this weekend that I will NEVER treat a player again the way I treated you on Friday night.

I recognized over that weekend that screaming at any child of any age was not coaching. That approach, yelling at a young person, was more about venting my own anger and frustration rather than addressing the honest mistake of a nervous 15-year-old. He simply lined up on the wrong side of the kicker.

By yelling at him the way I did, I diminished our overall program, I clearly broke this kid for the rest of this game (and maybe for a much longer time), and, in hindsight, I accomplished nothing in the process. In the end, the person who learned the most from this story was me. I learned that yelling is not an effective tool when coaching. As a coach, you may feel justified in yelling to get a point across, but in the long run, you undermine your own program.

Kids are fragile. The human spirit is fragile. Let's not break that spirit because a child makes a mistake on the field of play. It happens, and as a prepared coach, make plans NOW as to how you will react to the hundreds of mistakes you will see at this level. Don't react as I did as a young coach. No matter how long you have coached, know that you can learn something from year to year to make you better at your craft. Grow as a coach. Check your ego at the door. Focus on your kids and always ask yourself, how would you like to be treated if the roles were reversed? If that doesn't motivate you, how would you like your child to be treated if she or he was the one making the mistake? Remember, these are kids, and our overall goal is to make this a great sporting experience so the kids keep coming back year after year.

Here is a final observation about yelling: Nobody likes to be yelled at... period. But neither am I suggesting that kids be allowed to "walk all over you." Not at all. You are still in charge, and you are the coach/ teacher. Your need to have control of your practices and your games, which is no different than teachers who must have control of their classrooms to be an effective teacher. I get it. I respect it. And I also understand that some kids can get under your skin. But remember that coaching always comes down to two things: WHO you are (your character) and HOW you deliver your program! You are in charge. Raise the bar for yourself and those within your program. Together, you will create a wonderful sporting experience that every child and parent will want to reexperience when the next season rolls around.

Individual Win: I believe there are literally hundreds of "Individual Wins" taking place at every practice and game. Examples of Individual Wins:

- A good throw-in in soccer
- A good screen in basketball
- Being in the correct position for a rebound in basketball is an Individual Win even if there is no rebound
- A good outlet pass in hockey
- A good pass from the back row to the setter in volleyball
- A seamless passing of the baton in a relay race
- A good cutoff throw in baseball/softball
- A good pass route in football is an Individual Win even if the ball is not thrown to that receiver

The list could go on and on just like the number of Individual Wins.

Coaching goes far beyond the scoreboard. Are the kids learning the sport? Are the kids learning that everyone has a role on every play, including those on the bench? Speaking of being on the bench at some point during a game, are those kids (age appropriately) engaged with what is happening on the field? During a game or practice, I believe we must ensure that these kids all understand what is happening at any given time. Even though a child may not be in a specific play, they can certainly see what happened and listen for the coach to positively critique a given play or situation. Learning can and should be constantly happening even if a child is not on the field of play.

Unfortunately, that critique can cut both ways. If a coach ridicules a kid about a poor decision or a poor play, that coach's message will also be received by every one of the players (and probably not in an uplifting way). That is why focusing on the Individual Wins is so positive and so needed for everyone.

Kids want to hear uplifting critiques about their accomplishments, no matter how minor they may be. As a coach, you need not stop practice or become overly dramatic when complimenting an Individual Win; simply recognizing it and commenting on it will be heard *loud and clear* by every player. You are telling your players that you are paying attention to *everything* that is going on, and those observations may have nothing to do with the scoreboard. Most of the time, they do *not* have to do with the scoreboard. Here are a few stories that highlight the beauty of coaching Individual Wins and reacting to mistakes.

A sixth-grade boy is playing shortstop. The ball is hit right to him. The ball goes between his legs into left field. Who feels terrible about what just happened? The sixth-grade boy feels terrible. He made a mistake. How do some coaches respond after seeing a play like that? I have seen some coaches kick the screen while standing in the dugout or drop their clipboard in disgust or yell at the kid ("charge the ball" or "get down on the ball") or simply roll their eyes. The problem with all those reactions—not only do they do nothing to help that kid, but it also sends a message to the rest of the team that making a mistake is a huge disappointment to their coach.

In addition, because of the state of mind of that child at that time, he will not absorb and process anything the coach may have to say immediately after the miscue. Why? He is still feeling bad about making a mistake. In these situations, I advise coaches to try this approach:

"James, don't worry about that play. We now have a runner on first and two outs. Team, we now have a force-out at second base or a putout at first base. Let's focus on the next play."

As soon as there are three outs and James makes his way to the dugout, now is the time for you to teach/coach. James is no longer on the field for everyone to hear your instructions or frustrations. He is now in the safety of the dugout, and he will listen much more intently to whatever you want to convey to him.

You can say something fairly simple like, "James, let's charge those ground balls, make your crow-hop, and throw a strike to Tommy at first base. Errors are not a big deal. They happen. Forget about it. You are batting second this inning, so go get your bat and let's focus on making contact. Keep working hard."

As a sixth grader, James will not be able to articulate it, but he will appreciate how you handled his error, his mistake. How do you "deliver" your program? Check your competitive edge when you pull up for a practice or game. When you step out of your car, you become super teacher, not a loud coach correcting every mistake so forcefully that everyone in the immediate zip code can hear you. We acknowledge that you know the sport better than the kids. Now "deliver" your knowledge as a classroom teacher. I know you will. Thank you.

More Details on Individual Wins: Eighth-grade Girls Softball: Situation: 1 out, runner at first base. The ball is hit to left center. It appears that the left fielder may be able to catch the ball. The runner on first goes only halfway not knowing if the ball will be caught. The left fielder tries gallantly to get to the ball, but the ball gets by her. The center fielder is on her horse backing up the play and gets to the ball before it gets to the outfield wall. The runner on first is now approaching second base and will be heading to third base. Your shortstop knows what the runner is doing and aligns herself for the cutoff throw. The center fielder throws a strike to the shortstop (cutoff) and then the shortstop turns and fires a strike to third base. Your third baseperson makes a great catch and tag and the runner is... safe! If you are coaching the team on the field, you may be disappointed that the runner was not out. I can assure you that your parents are equally disappointed. However, let's count the Individual Wins in that one play:

1. Both outfielders broke on the ball as soon as it was hit.

2. The left fielder made a great attempt to catch the ball.

3. The center fielder backed up the play and kept the ball from getting to the fence.

4. The shortstop lined herself properly for the cutoff throw.

5. The center fielder hit the cutoff person by throwing a strike to the shortstop.

6. The shortstop caught the ball, turned, and threw a strike to third base.

7. The third baseperson caught the ball and put down an immediate tag.

8. The pitcher has backed up the throw to third base.

9. The second baseperson is covering second base in case the runner returned to second base or the batter/runner tries to go to second on the play at third base.

Which Individual Win do you want to focus on? There are at least nine Individual Wins by six different players taking place on that one play. How encouraging is that? You can praise them all for a great play. If your defensive team does not play that hard and know what to do, that close play at third is probably a run scored for the other team.

Here is another secret about those kinds of plays where your kids do everything perfectly but the call goes to the other team. It happens. It doesn't mean it was the wrong call—maybe the runner in this scenario is a great baserunner, saw what was happening, and got to third base a split second before the tag. So be it. What do your parents want badly on a play like this? They want the runner to be out! That is *their* only focus.

Here is the secret: You cannot coach like a parent spectates. The subtle difference is that parents focus on "results" (in this example, safe or out). Coaches need to focus on "process." Look at all the GREAT things that had to happen to make this a close play at third base. Safe or out, you get to congratulate your players for at least nine great things that happened on that one play.

There are literally hundreds of Individual Wins taking place at every practice and game, and our job as a coach is to recognize an Individual Win and reward it—not necessarily over-the-top praise. A quick "Nice job. I saw what you did there. Way to go" can be both that simple and that powerful. It will be heard by every player. If you effectively coach Individual Wins, these kids will run through a wall for you. It is highly effective, and it has nothing to do with the scoreboard. If you effectively coach the Individual Wins, the scoreboard will take care of itself.

One more example: Fifth-grade Girls Basketball: You are coaching the team bringing the ball down the court (offensive possession). Your kids do a great job of moving the ball; several quality passes occur. Finally, the ball ends up in Hannah's hands, and she shoots and makes a 3-pointer!

The parents go crazy, Hannah is pumped, and your team is running back to set up on defense. As the coach, you noticed that as Hannah set up to shoot the 3-pointer, her teammate Madeline got herself in perfect position for a rebound, but there was, of course, no rebound. Hannah hit the 3-pointer.

As the kids are running back to set up on defense, you have the wonderful opportunity to congratulate Hannah on her 3-pointer. "Hannah, nice shot, well done." However, you also have the equally wonderful opportunity to congratulate Madeline for getting herself in the perfect position for a rebound even though there was no rebound to be had. "Madeline, I saw you get yourself in a perfect rebound position. Nice job, well done!"

Madeline never touched the ball, but I guarantee you that Madeline will position herself correctly every time a shot goes up because she knows you are watching. Recognizing Individual Wins *is* coaching. You can't get caught watching the ball all the time. Most of the game is happening away from the ball. Look for opportunities to reward Individual Wins. It is such a positive and effective way of coaching.

Individual Wins – What Are They?

- There are many Individual Wins, by all players, taking place on every play of every game and practice, even if kids are not directly involved in the play.

- Our job is to take our attention off the scoreboard (or the result of the play) and put it on the Individual Wins. There are far more Individual Wins taking place than there are points on the scoreboard. Coaches, if you concentrate more on the Individual Wins, the scoreboard will take care of itself.

- Individual Wins happen when we help kids think about their successes and failures in ways that build self-esteem.

- Focusing on Individual Wins is a very **proactive** approach to coaching as opposed to **reactive** or results-oriented coaching.

- Parents concern themselves with **results**; coaches must concern themselves with **process.**

- Don't let the scoreboard become the only barometer of your efforts and the children's efforts. Yes, winning is more fun than losing. However, if winning is your *only* goal or your primary goal, then I suggest you reconsider coaching our children. Move to the high school varsity level or the college level or the professional level. At the grade school level and early high school level, I believe our goals are:

  - To make the experience as enjoyable as possible;

- As best you can, develop all the children on your roster;

- As best you can, share your passion for the game;

- Age appropriately, teach the fundamentals, tactics, and strategies of the game.

- And finally, make this activity such a positive experience that these children keep coming out to participate in youth sports year after year.

Regardless of your win-loss record, I believe **Individual Wins** can drive your program.

Two Steps to Coaching Individual Wins

1. **Recognize and reinforce successes** – Successes are taking place all over the field or court, even if the child is not directly involved in the play. **Notice** when he or she might be disappointed.

2. **Give the right kind of feedback** – The **time** you choose to give your feedback is as critical as the feedback itself. Give thought to your timing, as each child will require a slightly different approach based on his or her personality.

- Empathize. Show them you understand how they might be feeling.

- Tell the truth (with charity). Let them have their own experience, including disappointment.

- Help them explain disappointments and failures realistically.

I believe that it is not just successes and failures that affect a child's self-esteem, but **how they think** about their successes and failures.

Chapter 7

In-Season Checklist, Practice Pyramid, and Discipline

Coaching Coaches Pyramid – In-Season Checklist, Practice Pyramid, and Discipline

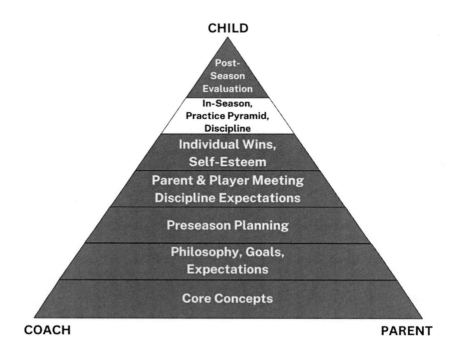

CHILD

Post-Season Evaluation

In-Season, Practice Pyramid, Discipline

Individual Wins, Self-Esteem

Parent & Player Meeting Discipline Expectations

Preseason Planning

Philosophy, Goals, Expectations

Core Concepts

COACH   **PARENT**

In-Season Checklist, Practice Pyramid, and Discipline: Coaches, you are clearly into your season. Practices have begun, and games are just around the corner or may have already begun. How is it going?

The In-Season Checklist is provided in full later in this chapter. Here are a few thoughts about your In-Season Checklist: Make sure you have your Coach's Binder with you always. That binder should contain contact information for all the kids and their parents, rules and regulations from your association, your sport's rules and policies, contact information for your sport directors and/or your organization's board members, and the "permission to treat forms" in the event something really goes wrong and a child has to go to the urgent care or the hospital and you cannot get a hold of the parents (I have never had to use this form, but I always have it with me).

Though not every organization has a "permission to treat" policy/form, having a signed permission form for each child can be highly beneficial in the event of a medical crisis.

Further, having permission forms for your players communicates to their parents that you are prepared for any situation. Your first and foremost concern about this season is the safety, health, and well-being of your players, and the items that you bring to each practice and game reflect those concerns.

You not only have your coach's binder on hand always, but to *every* practice and game you bring a first aid kit and a small cooler with ice and large and small zip lock bags to be used as necessary. I jokingly tell coaches during my coaching presentations that as prepared as I was in the event of a medical issue on the field, my first aid kit was used mostly by the parents for little siblings who got stung by a bee while hanging around the garbage cans! In the first aid kit, I carried bee sting kits, which were used more than anything else.

Finally, do you have any kids with allergies (food or otherwise)? Please have individual conversations with those parents so that both you and your assistants understand the allergy and what to do if an issue arises. Also, if you have parents bring after-the-game snacks, do these parents understand that you might have a child or two with a food allergy?

All this information must be communicated. Believe it or not, that is a part of saying "yes" to coaching at this level. I know it sounds tedious; some of you might be thinking, "I didn't sign up for all of this. I just want to coach a sport." The truth is, at this level, you are the coach, the trainer, the media contact, and in some ways, the athletic director.

Don't let this part overwhelm you. Yes, it can feel overwhelming, but the goal here is to be as prepared as you can in the event you encounter an issue. Your chances of having a catastrophic injury or accident are very, very low. However, if you have spent some time preparing properly for the possibility of injuries or allergies, every parent will feel good about having you as their coach. It is a part of building a program and having a process. You are on the *top of your game*. Thanks, Coach! Nice Job!

Coach's In-Season Checklist

This document is designed to be used during the season to keep you on task and remind you of your coaching responsibilities.

1. Have your coach's binder, first aid kit, ice, and plastic bags that lock at all practices and games.

2. Prepare for all your practices and games using the Practice Pyramid, your stated philosophies, goals, and expectations. **Be prepared tactically and emotionally every time you step onto the field or court.**

3. Adjust the length of all the sections based on the age of the kids you are coaching.

4. Continue to seek effective drills, via books, the internet, or clinics, that you think will be effective for your team, keeping in mind your players' ages and abilities. Remember, you can make up any drill you want.

5. Continue to seek knowledge of what to expect from your players regarding physical and mental capabilities. As a generalization, we would all hope to coach the "best" kids, but most coaches will be coaching a wide variety of skill levels.

6. Stay with your players after all practices and games to make sure they have all been picked up safely. Ask your parents to **not** drop off their children and leave until a coach has shown up. **No matter the situation, never leave kids of any age by themselves**. This is probably the greatest responsibility we have to the children and their families. Finally, avoid being left one-on-one with a child waiting for a parent. Insist that another coach or parent wait with you or ask the second-to-last pickup to wait with you and the last child to be picked up until his or her parent arrives.

7. Have your **actions** constantly communicate your philosophies, goals, and expectations throughout the season. After all the letters go out, it is your **actions** that will dictate your **real** philosophies, goals, and expectations.

8. Continue to communicate throughout the season. This kind of effort reinforces your commitment to each family. Please don't let this slide.

9. Continue to review your rule book.

10. Continue to keep your coach's binder up-to-date.

11. **Have fun. Enjoy the experience. You are organized and effective. Nice job, Coach!!**

The Practice Pyramid

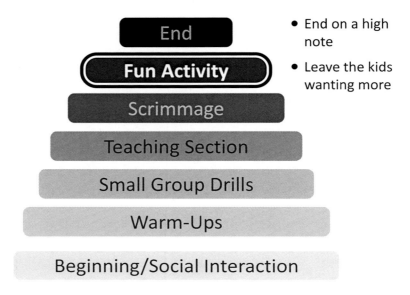

- End on a high note
- Leave the kids wanting more

The Practice Pyramid is designed to give the coach a skeletal view of an organized practice. The objective is to keep the practice organized, focused, and **fun** and to provide the highest return of productivity for the shortest amount of time. Don't forget to incorporate breaks into your practice and adjust all the times based on the age group you are coaching.

Explanation of the Practice Pyramid

- **A beginning and an end** – There is always a beginning and an end. This technique adds structure and continuity to practices.

- **The warm-up** – The warm-up tells the players that practice has begun and emphasizes that all players should get into the habit of warming up and stretching prior to a strenuous activity (8 to 10 minutes).

- **Small group drills** – This section is designed for the players to work on their individual skills. Try to have three or four drill stations prepared, and rotate the players throughout the drills in approximately 5- to 6-minute increments. This will keep the players busy and focused working on their individual skills. Keep the drills age-appropriate for your players' skill level (16 to 20 minutes total).

- **The teaching section** – This is the time in practice where you want to discuss one, two, or three teaching points. This could be new material or observations from the previous game or practice. Be very prepared for this section and try to keep it concise and to the point (10 to 15 minutes; less for younger players).

- **Scrimmage** – This is the section where you allow your players to scrimmage. Try to make it as competitive, game like, and **fun** as possible. The players don't want to practice drills the entire time, and they don't want to be taught (spoken to) all practice. **They want to play.** As a coach, remember **why** these kids signed up in the first place. They want to have **fun** and **play** the sport (20 minutes).

- **Fun activity** – Your practice is now coming to an end, and you want to end with another fun activity but always teaching. You are leaving the players on a high note. You are leaving the players wanting more (5 to 7 minutes).

- **The end** – The end is made up of announcements. This is where you praise a good practice, take care of any administrative needs, make any announcements, distribute any handouts, etc. Remember, have a beginning and an end. This establishes a flow and continuity to your practices.

Note: Adjust the length of all the sections based on the age of the players you are coaching. Also, make sure you provide enough water breaks based on the weather conditions. Use good common sense when it comes to adverse conditions, especially adverse weather conditions. Thank you.

Reminder: As a coach, do not leave the field or court until all players have been picked up safely!! Thank you again!

Practice Pyramid: How do you effectively prepare for a practice? My practice pyramid is designed to give a coach an overview of how a prepared practice can give a team the most amount of learning in the shortest amount of time.

What is your ROI ("Return on Investment") for every practice? Depending on the age of the kids, you are regularly investing between 30 and 90 minutes per practice. What are you and your team getting back for that investment of time?

The answer lies with every individual coach. How prepared are you? How efficient are you during practice? How much fun are the kids having? How well is your classroom (field or court) being run?

Preparation. Preparation. Preparation. It all begins with how well prepared you are for *every* practice. I used to schedule my practices down to the minute. Being that prepared made the practice run more smoothly and delivered a message to the kids that even though we are here to have fun and enjoy the experience, we are also here to learn the tactics and strategies of a given sport.

In addition, it sets a tone for the entire season. This is your classroom. How is it going to be run? I am looking for you to put your best foot forward and make the best of your practice time. Ideally, at the end of practice, the kids will tell their parents on the ride home that practice was great and they can't wait to get back to it. How cool is that? That alone is a huge WIN for you and your program!

What are the specifics of a well-run practice? We have already established that preparing your practice in the car on the way to practice is no way to prepare. We've also established that because you played a given sport 10, 15, 20, or 25 years ago, you "know what you are doing" or "these are only second graders or sixth graders or eighth graders. I know more than they do," is not valid preparation either.

Every practice is unique. Every team is unique. Every coach is unique. I have broken my practice pyramid into seven sections: Beginning/

Social Interaction, Warm-Ups, Small Group Drills, Teaching Section, Scrimmage, Fun Activity, and End of Practice.

Beginning/Social Interaction: I hope all the coaches are the *first* people to show up for practice. As a team of coaches, take five to ten minutes to discuss what is going to happen over the course of your practice. Who is going to be responsible for what? This is also a good time to set up cones or complete any other preparation required prior to your practice beginning. You are now all set as the kids start to arrive. All coaches should greet each child. Make it a happy greeting. You should be honestly happy that the kids have arrived at practice. Engage the parents whether they are simply dropping off kids or whether they are staying for the practice.

Engage with the kids. How was your day? How was school today? Any tests? What subjects do you like best? I hear you have a new baby sister... how is that going? How is your mom doing? How is your dad doing? The goal here is to let your kids know that no matter how young they are, you are interested in them as a person and not just as a player.

Warm-Ups: After you have met with your coaches, welcomed the kids, and the start time for practice is upon you, gather the kids and start with a series of age-appropriate warm-ups. At the youth sports level, the warm-up, though important, does not have to be aggressive, as their young muscles are already very flexible. An equally important factor in the warm-up is the subtle message you are sending, which is: PRACTICE HAS BEGUN!!

For any classroom, you have a START and a FINISH. The warm-up is your start of practice even if all the kids are not there. START ON TIME! If kids are late, the kids will be upset with their parents, not you. In fact, they will not want to be late again, so they will pester their parents to get them there on time.

In your preseason meeting, explain this to your parents. That is, we will start *on* time, *every* time. Your warm-up need not be lengthy. The older kids may require some more intense warm-up, but you can make the call on that. No effective teacher tolerates silliness once class has begun. There is a line between silliness and enjoying the experience. Silliness and inappropriate behavior ends while my class is going on. Set that expectation, not as a drill sergeant, but as a competent teacher of your sport. Regardless of their age, we are going to be teaching something at every practice. That is why we are the coach/teacher!

Small Group Drills: Social interaction has come and gone. You have age appropriately warmed up your kids to start your practice. Now it is time to start throwing the ball, hitting the ball, passing the ball, shooting the ball, passing the puck, passing the baton, or working on your latest wrestling move. Small group drills are designed to focus your kids on the "skills and drills" of your sport in the shortest amount of time.

Small group drills are designed to create as many "touches" as possible, regardless of your sport. The kids are focused. They get plenty of opportunities to improve their individual performances, and they strive to master a skill. (We will come back to mastering a drill shortly.) In addition, if you set up three or four stations, each child can concentrate on an individual station for some 5 to 6 minutes and then move on to the next station.

Let's look at the benefits of small group drills. First, the kids are focused on their individual performance. They are engaged. They are trying to master this age-appropriate skill. While kids are getting multiple touches of the ball (or whatever your sport requires), your potential discipline issues fall to about zero!

This is another reason that I encourage all coaches to get as many assistant coaches as you can so that at every practice you can assign one adult for each drill. This structure keeps the practice moving and keeps your players and coaches engaged. If you are the head coach, the more assistants you can incorporate into your program, the better. Maybe a parent has never coached a sport and all they want to do is to run one drill and be an expert on that drill. Great! Encourage and teach your inexperienced coaches just as you teach your kids. You can help educate multiple people at the same time.

Once your coaches start to gain confidence, they will beat you to practice! I had a softball team of 14 girls for several years (fifth thru eighth grade), and we had seven coaches (me and six assistants). Our practices looked like a college program. We had multiple drills going on simultaneously: infield practice, outfield practice, hitting practice, pitching practice, and base-running practice. We could get through a meaningful and upbeat practice in about 70 minutes with breaks and never had a discipline issue. In fact, the kids could not wait to get back to practice. That is when you know you've captured their interest and imagination. They can't wait to get back to practice.

With seven adults helping and an organized practice that is preplanned, everyone on that softball team got multiple touches at every drill. And they received multiple accolades at every station. Why wouldn't they want to come back?

Create an environment that says, this is the place to be! It is fun, they are learning, they are getting many compliments, and the time flies by. One of your goals is to create the BEST hours of the week for your kids. And that occurs because of WHO you are and HOW you deliver your program.

Some coaches find drills on the internet and want to incorporate ALL of them in their practices. Please do not do this. Pick out maybe four to six small group drills that are age-appropriate for your kids and allow your kids to master each drill. If you keep changing the drills, it can create frustration because the kids are not seeing the skill acquisition that they want and need to see. This would be akin to a piano teacher providing a child with a piece of music and never letting them master that music before quickly moving onto another piece. Find a small amount of age-appropriate drills and focus repeatedly on those drills. Though you can find thousands of drills for any sport on the internet, you don't need all of them. A few well-chosen drills will suffice for your team.

Here is another trick when it comes to picking drills: Think about the sport you are coaching and develop your OWN DRILLS! I used to create my own drills and made sure that my drills were as game like as possible. Think through small scenarios about what happens in the sport you are coaching.

In soccer, for instance, do you have a throw-in drill? How many throw-ins happen during a soccer match? There are numerous throw-ins throughout the course of a match. Why not replicate that specific play during your practices?

For the older kids, come up with some "throw-in" plays. Have players switch throwing and receiving the ball, sometimes throw the ball backward, and always try to get your kids to throw the ball in quickly, to catch the other team unprepared. This one drill, "throw-ins," may happen 10 to 20 times in a child's game. Create a drill around this most common occurrence in the game of soccer. After some practice, your kids will treat throw-ins like shooting on goal; they will want to throw in the ball (or defend properly on a throw-in). They will have mastered a huge part of the game.

You can help them create a competitive advantage, and it all begins with a well-thought-out drill involving throw-ins with as few as three to five kids at that one station for 5 to 6 minutes. If you conduct that drill over and over for several weeks, you will see huge improvement by every player. It is fun to watch.

What will be the four to six drills that will accurately replicate your sport? Think about it. Be creative and don't be afraid to go back to the drawing board if a drill is not successful, is too difficult, or results in unanticipated player frustration. You may have to work at it a little bit, but over time, you will tweak your drills, and you will find them a huge success.

Also, know that at the beginning of the season, you must explain each drill to both the coaches and the players. That will slow things down at the beginning of the season, but after a few practices, the drills will become more comfortable, and the kids will focus on proficiency.

Here is another helpful tip: Once you get some assistant coaches (one or more), have a short coaches-only session to review drills and the overall practice strategy. At this session, you can review the teaching points of each drill, and you can assign drills or maybe even rotate the coaches so they all learn the finer points of each drill. The purpose of this session is to "coach the coaches."

Teaching Section: So, what have we done so far? You have happily welcomed the kids and their parents to your practice. You have put the kids through age-appropriate warm-ups. You have prepared and executed the Small Group Drills section. You are approximately a third of the way through your practice. Now is the time to plan a short portion of your practice to TEACH! Spread the kids out so they are not touching each other or playing around. Kids' attention spans are short; know what specific points you want to get across to your team during this practice and explain everything as concisely as you can.

Also, be prepared to demonstrate your teaching points. Most kids (and adults) are VISUAL learners. We can all benefit from seeing what you are talking about. As examples, players (and parents) often do not understand off-sides in soccer or the three-second lane violation in basketball or the infield fly rule in baseball and softball or how the rotation works in volleyball.

Make your teaching section powerful, concise, and focused. You don't have to teach all the finer points of your sport in one or two practices. Review the age of your kids that you will be coaching and decide the number of skills and strategies that you want to TEACH your kids throughout the entire season. For younger kids, that may only be five or six things for the entire season. For the older kids, that may be 12 to 20 things that you want to teach them throughout the course of the entire season.

Prior to the season, discuss all of this with your assistant coaches and get buy-in from them regarding your teaching plans. They may have some input that you may not have thought about. And they will feel like they are more than a "drill coach." Your assistants will feel more involved, and they will feel like they are truly an assistant coach, as they should. Remember that coaching at any level goes far beyond the skills and drills of the game. As a head coach, you are responsible for bringing everyone together (you, assistant coaches, kids, parents, grandparents, and other family members). You are the ringmaster, and the more you communicate with everyone in your tent, the better experience everyone will have during your season.

Scrimmage: Here is where the greatest fun of your practice will take place; you allow the kids to scrimmage. Try to make this time as competitive, as game like, and as fun as possible. The kids don't want to practice drills for the entire time, and they don't want to be taught (spoken to) all practice. THEY WANT TO PLAY! As a volunteer coach, remember why these kids signed up in the first place. They want to have fun and enjoy PLAYING the sport. Please don't lose sight of that most important part of coaching.

For about 5 years, I coached 14 girls on our soccer team. They were great kids, we had great assistant coaches, and we were blessed with great parents. When this team got to the scrimmage part of the practice, they were pumped up and ready to go. It was a game like atmosphere. It was competitive. They were focused and ready to play hard. It is always hard to simulate game conditions, but we came close to doing just that. Our scrimmages were not just fun time. It was a learning experience for everyone, and we had a winner and a loser.

With only 14 players, how do you simulate a soccer game? First, we cut the field in half, creating a 50-yard field. At one end was the actual goal, and in the middle of the field (50 yards from that goal) were about 10 cones, stretching from sideline to sideline, which represented the other end line for our scrimmage purposes. (You can adjust the length of the field based on the age of your team.) One team consisted of four players: a goalie and three "stoppers" in front of the actual goal. The other team consisted of 10 players. Yes, that's right, it was 10 v 4!

The team with 10 players does *not* have a goalie or an actual goal. They are defending the 8 to 10 cones stretching from sideline to sideline. They have all the other 10 positions covered but no goalie. Here is how the scoring worked: The team with 10 players received one point for every goal they could score against the three stoppers and the one goalie. However, the team with only four players (the goalie and the three stoppers) scored two points if they could simply clear the ball beyond the 8 to 10 cones that divided the field in half. They only had to kick the ball past the cones. If they could do that, they got two points!

When these rules were introduced, an interesting dynamic occurred. The four defense-only kids worked tirelessly to find an opening and clear the ball past the cones at midfield to earn their two points. In addition, they worked diligently to defend their goal. They gave us a real look regarding what we would experience on game days when we applied offensive pressure. The four were as competitive as they could be. We freely changed some of the four players during the scrimmage just for fun. A kid could go from the winning team to the losing team and vice versa. This was not a big deal, as they wanted to perform well regardless of which team they played on.

Offensively, the 10 kids who made up the other team experienced something quite different. With only four defenders, the 10 could frequently experience a series of successful "give and go's," successful passing to space, successful throw-ins, and successful ball control. Kids need to experience what success feels like beyond just scoring a goal.

In addition, they did *not* want to lose to the team of four! Plus, the defenders on the team of 10 would have to run extremely hard to make sure a ball did *not* get past the cones at midfield. They knew that if the ball got by them and the cones, it cost their team two points. It created great competitiveness for *every* player regardless of which team they were on. They loved it.

All the players competed incredibly hard, and I would only stop the play periodically, for maybe 5 to 10 seconds, to explain a coaching point (I was quick and to the point) and then we would play on. We put the scrimmage on a clock, and when it was winding down, we would start to count the time down to zero. It was very intense and great fun!

I did not find this scrimmage concept in a book or on the internet. I created it because I thought it would give us what our team needed. Get creative. You can do something similar with your team and your sport. We only scrimmaged for about 20 minutes, but it was truly effective; every player had multiple touches of the ball and took great pride in their contributions. (Side note: Adjust your scrimmage as needed and, as always, make your scrimmage age-appropriate.)

Fun Activity: At this point, the practice is just about over. You have allowed the kids to warm up effectively, to practice their individual skills, to absorb some concepts via the teaching section, and to have great fun by providing an intense and focused scrimmage.

Remember, the goal is to create a high-tempo/high-energy practice and execute the entire practice in a short period of time. Get 'em in, get 'em out, and see you later. This strategy isn't callous; rather, it achieves the overarching goal of keeping them wanting more. I wanted my kids thinking to themselves as they leave the field, "I can't wait to get back to practice." In fact, parents often reported that their child said those exact words on the way home from practice. That is exactly what you want: high-energy, well-organized, short practices!

Since your practice is nearly over, end on as high a note as you can. I used to end my practices with some creative way to be competitive, learn something, and to move fast. Win or lose, the fun activity is designed to end your practices on a high note! We often organized relay races or ball-handling skill races or just some silly relay race (maybe carry several soccer balls from one set of cones to another and then hand the balls off to your teammate and then have the receiver run to the far end carrying all the soccer balls). The players always engaged energetically with a lot of screaming and yelling. It was a great way to end practice. End on a high note!

End of Practice: Even though the official practice is over, please take 3 to 5 minutes and gather both the kids and the parents and make announcements, praise their good work, announce any administrative requests, distribute any handouts, and certainly confirm the next practice or game details. Now you can dismiss everyone. Once again, you have a beginning (greeting the kids at the beginning of the practice) and an end of the practice (dismissing everyone after your announcements). A formal beginning and formal end. Just like a classroom! **FINALLY, WHETHER IT IS YOU OR AN ASSIGNED ASSISTANT COACH, DO NOT LEAVE YOUR PRACTICE AREA UNTIL ALL THE KIDS HAVE BEEN PICKED UP SAFELY!**

Revisiting the 7 Steps to Discipline: I realize we addressed some specifics of discipline in Chapter 5 as you prepared for your parent/ player preseason meeting, but I want to cover it again because you are now into the season and the potential for discipline issues becomes a reality. Those 7 steps are a great outline for you to review prior to any practice or game, and it is hugely important that your assistant coaches and parents are on the same page with you when it comes to discipline. Addressing the issue of discipline BEFORE you have an issue makes all the difference. For these 7 Steps to Discipline to be effective, everyone (including the kids) must understand the 7 steps and accept any consequences associated with acting out at a practice or game. The greatest asset to a discipline plan is thorough communication! Let me share a coaching insight regarding discipline: When I was coaching, I can honestly tell you that very few discipline issues arose. Why? I made my discipline plan exceedingly clear. I was very upfront and set an expectation for myself, my assistant coaches, my players, and my parents.

In addition, I was highly organized when it came to both practices and games. The more organized I was, the fewer discipline issues I encountered. Remember, when practices are highly organized, well executed, and efficiently quick, the kids do not have time to get into trouble. Things are moving too fast, and they are too focused.

Incorporate the 7 Steps to Discipline judiciously, and your need to invoke disciplinary action will be limited. You cannot be an effective teacher if you are constantly battling discipline issues.

Revisiting the 7 Steps to Discipline

1. The more you are organized in all phases of your coaching, the fewer problems you will have.

2. Develop a philosophy of behavior that you expect, then communicate it clearly and often to both the players and their parents.

3. Prepare yourself to handle discipline problems in a low-key manner and institute a matter-of-fact approach. Remember, most discipline problems are the result of a child not getting enough attention either from you or his or her peers.

4. Once a low-key warning has been given to a child or group of children and the child or group continues to act up, a simple time-out away from all the other kids is appropriate (approximately 5 minutes). **Make sure to keep the child or children within your sight if this action is taken.**

   - It can also be very effective to address the inappropriate behavior in a one-on-one setting, with another coach in attendance so you are not considered "alone" with the child.

5. If a child (or group of children) demonstrates an ongoing discipline problem, you have attempted to discipline the child with time-outs, you have talked to the child one-on-one, and you still see no improvement, get the parents involved **immediately**. Solicit the parents' help and form an alliance with the parents to resolve the issue.

6. If you do not get the appropriate support from the parents, you may have no choice but to seek the director of your sport and/or the board of your organization for help. You cannot be an effective coach if you are constantly battling discipline problems. **It just won't work!**

7. Remember steps No. 1 and No. 2: The more you are organized in all phases of your coaching, the fewer problems you will have. Develop a philosophy of behavior that you

expect, then communicate it clearly and often to both the players and their parents.

- A final thought: Work hard to avoid sarcasm. The younger players don't understand your "shot," and the older players become embarrassed and will build walls that may never come down.

Weather Conditions

There is no governing body to oversee the weather conditions for youth sports except for when lightning is in the area and a park ranger stops your play. In some cases, that might not happen. Coaches, it is your responsibility to monitor extreme weather conditions:

Heat
- Heat indexes at or above 90 degrees

Cold
- Wind chills at or below 32 degrees

For many coaches, you reflect "back in the day" and say, "I was outside in those types of weather conditions, and it didn't hurt me" or something along those lines. It was always hotter and/or colder, and you are better for it. Personally, I hated the extreme weather conditions, and I am clearly not better for it. I have very sensitive toes from playing hockey in subzero weather for hours at a time. I never performed as well in extreme heat; I don't think anyone does. It wears you down.

The point is simple: **Use good judgment.** You will not jeopardize a child's college scholarship because you canceled a practice or two when they were 5, 7, 9, 11, or 13 years old. The parents will love you, and the players will appreciate the break. We run their sports back-to-back anyway, so an unexpected break will help their mental attitude toward you and your program, and you will clearly be doing what is in the best interest of the child.

If you do move forward with a practice or a game in extreme weather, make sure you are overly prepared for any situation. By not canceling a practice or a game because of extreme weather, you have now put the players, yourself, your staff, and your fans at some additional risk. Be mindful of these possibilities when making your decision. Below are some additional precautions:

Extreme heat or cold precautions

- Allow for several water breaks.
- Have water on demand.
- Be conscious of heat exhaustion and/or heat stroke.
- Be conscious of frostbite.

Finally, **do not attempt to outrun lightning.** I have seen lightning hit near players, and it is scary! I tell people I am (or was) fairly fast, but I am clearly not that fast. Lightning kills. Use your **best** judgment when lightning is in the area!

Thank you for taking this section very seriously. You ARE the governing body. It always comes down to your good common sense. Be smart and be player safe!

Chapter 8

Postseason Evaluation

Coaching Coaches Pyramid – Postseason Evaluation

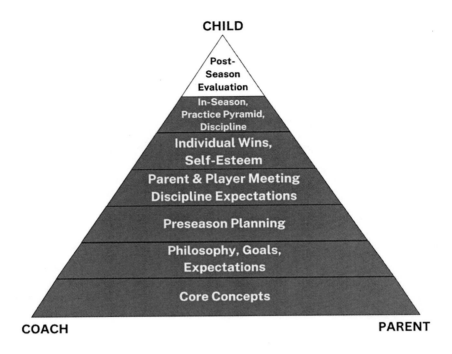

CHILD

Post-Season Evaluation

In-Season, Practice Pyramid, Discipline

Individual Wins, Self-Esteem

Parent & Player Meeting Discipline Expectations

Preseason Planning

Philosophy, Goals, Expectations

Core Concepts

COACH   PARENT

Postseason Evaluation: Coaches, we discussed in the introduction that coaching at any level has a preseason, in-season, and postseason. We have covered the preseason and in-season activities/ checklist, and now it is time to focus on the postseason activities.

Not unexpectedly, the postseason section of this book is the least-read section. Why? Because most busy coaches finish a season and then quickly move onto the next upcoming season or activity. But I would suggest that when all is said and done, the postseason exercises in this section may most strongly affect *your* development as a coach. Why? Most coaches *never* assess their own performance. I will say that again: I believe most coaches *never* assess their own performance. Most people are too busy, and sadly, some coaches can't wait for the season to be over.

Your greatest chance of improvement as a coach comes from those first days immediately *after* the end of your season. Your just-completed season is still fresh in your mind. You probably still have some energy and enthusiasm about your season. This is the time to ask yourself, "How did it go?" This is the opportunity to reflect on some three or four months of work (teaching/coaching), parent meetings, practices, games, some possible discipline issues, some possible parent issues, and some possible conflicts with an assistant coach, an opposing coach, or with an official. Good or bad, exhilarating or disheartening, it's important that you evaluate the entire season: preseason, in-season, and postseason.

Once the practices and the games have stopped, it is hard to get motivated to assess your own performance. However, it will be one of the best things you can do for yourself and your team as you mentally start preparing for the next year. That is why I ask you to assess your own performance within a few days of the end of the current season while your memories are still strong. Additionally, I can pretty much assure you that no one within your athletic organization will conduct a postseason review with you. You are very much on your own.

As difficult as it may be, I believe you must assess your own performance as best you can. You owe it to your kids, your parents, your assistant coaches, your organization, and yourself. We only get better at our craft if we honestly assess the pros and cons of the season.

The good news is that your program effectiveness will increase from year to year because you took the time to assess your strengthens and weaknesses. Completing this honest self-study will put you in a much better position to take your program to an even higher level next year.

Teaching/coaching is a process. Once you adopt the practice of postseason evaluation, you'll benefit from improvement in every phase of your program.

We can all tweak our programs to improve the overall experience for *everyone* involved, and it all starts with YOU! My Coach's Postseason Checklist asks you some 30 questions about your season. Remember that no one will ever see your responses. The whole objective with this exercise is to pick up the mirror and honestly assess whether you helped create a good experience for everyone associated with your program. I confidently believe the answer to that question for most of you is "yes"! Time spent completing this postseason assessment will make your program an even better experience as you move forward throughout your coaching years.

Speaking for each of your kids, your parents, your assistant coaches, and your organization, thank you so much for humbly and honestly completing this postseason exercise. I am confident that this exercise will truly improve your program from year to year.

Coach's Postseason Checklist

This checklist is designed to assist a coach in assessing his or her coaching performance. Any coach who goes through this process will be a better coach from year to year because he or she has taken the time to reflect on the season.

1. **Congratulations!** You finished the season! Were you proud of your performance as a leader?
2. Did you or your organization distribute an evaluation form to the families?
3. Did the kids have **fun**?
4. Did you see individual improvement?
5. Did you have **fun**?
6. Were you pleased with your philosophies, goals, and expectations? What changes will you make, if any? How did you do regarding "Individual Wins"?
7. Did you review the 7 Steps to Discipline, develop a plan for discipline, and communicate your plan to the kids and parents?
8. Did you remind yourself, before each practice and game, that you are the adult helping to administer a child's game?
9. Did you consistently prepare for your practices and games?
10. Did you incorporate **fun** into your practices and games?
11. How do you think you did regarding yelling vs. teaching? As you review the roster, how many players will probably sign up again next year. If you think that you have players who will not sign up next year, ask yourself why? (At various ages, some players discover that a given sport is not for them. However, there may be others who will not sign up again because of the experience—what about them?)
12. Did you host a parent/player meeting?
13. Did you effectively communicate, on a regular basis, with the families?

14. Did you review your Preseason and In-Season Checklist?

15. Did you keep your coach's binder updated all season long?

16. Did you bring a first aid kit, ice, and locking plastic bags to every practice and game? Did you seek out first aid, CPR, and AED classes?

17. Officials – How did you do working with the officials? Remember, our young officials are learning how to officiate and could use your understanding, your help, and your empathy. Please treat all officials with respect; please treat our young officials as if they were your own children. **Thank you!**

18. Did you think at some point during the season you were:

   a. An inspired leader?

   b. An educator?

   c. A psychologist?

   d. Approachable?

   e. A communicator?

   f. Organized?

   g. Setting a positive tone?

   h. Coordinating several things at once?

   i. Showing empathy?

   j. Setting expectations?

   k. Consistent?

   l. Creative?

   m. Showing concern by contacting a family after an injury?

   n. Having fun?

   o. Making a **positive difference** in a child's life?

Coach Summary

Thanks for taking the time to evaluate your performance. Coaching is a **process** that continually evolves. Some days you and the kids can't do anything wrong; other days you and the kids can't seem to do anything right! Work to rise above the discouragements and remind yourself that coaching is no different than teaching in a classroom. It takes time to be effective. It takes time to develop your own coaching style. It takes time to build a program! Be assured that the clear majority of the players and parents truly appreciate your efforts.

Keep assessing your performance, and you will become the kind of coach that all players and parents desire. You are well on your way to making a positive difference in a child's life!

Great job, Coach, and thank you!

Chapter 9

**Suggested Strategies in
Support of Child Safety**

Coaches, as much as we focus on organization, planning, teaching, age-appropriate drills, having fun, and expectations, your foremost concern must be the safety of your kids and your families! The chances of something ugly happening under your watch are very small, but that doesn't excuse you from considering and planning for a safety emergency. Treat this issue the way you would treat your favorite drill. Put time and effort into it. Make it a priority. Make sure it is a part of your parent/player preseason meeting. Be consistent with your approach to your child safety program. If you address this issue seriously, I can guarantee that your parents and kids will treat it seriously as well.

Strategies for Coaches in Support of Child Safety

- Age-appropriately, develop and implement a Buddy System for all teams. Use a minimum of two parents when implementing a Buddy System:

  - To and from restrooms

  - To and from concession stands

  - Going to a playground area prior to or after your practices or games

- During your parent/player meeting, explain how important each child's safety is to you, your assistants, and your program. Seek help from the parents from day one with this most important issue. Thank you!

- Make sure that **you** and **all** your assistants fill out the proper paperwork for a background check. Demand this of yourself and your assistants, even if your organization does not make it mandatory.

If your organization provides a Child Safety program, please require that program for yourself and your assistants. If possible, get parents to attend as well.

Chapter 10

Bommaritoisms

The following are short thoughts and strategies that I have applied to coaching youth sports. Maybe some will resonate with you and motivate you to get as creative as you would like. Coaches, thanks again for coaching our kids!

Bommarito's Golden Rule: Coaching always comes down to two things: **WHO** you are (your character) and **HOW** you deliver your program.

Assigned Roles: Remember these four roles during every practice and game. We all have a role: Kids are there to play, coaches are there to coach, officials are there to officiate, and fans are there to support. The only time we have issues in youth sports is when someone does **NOT** play their role effectively or wants to play a different role.

What Is a Youth Coach's Number One Goal? I believe the primary goal of every coach at the youth level is to create the best possible sporting experience for every child, parent, and coach so that all children sign up again next year. *Winning is a bonus at this level.* Winning is not the primary reason we coach at the youth level. *Education and a positive experience, from year to year, is the goal.* If you, as the coach, do not create a positive and enjoyable experience, I can assure you many children will not sign up for the next season, and—guess what?—you will not be able to teach them anything. They won't be there.

Preseason Planning and Execution: Many a season is won or lost before the children ever step on the field of play. Get your act together and, with great enthusiasm, deliver your program!

Parent/Player Meeting: Preparing for and executing an effective preseason parent/player meeting is as important to your program as teaching any aspect of your sport.

Parent/Player Meeting: The wisdom of an effective preseason parent/player meeting is this: The season has NOT begun, and the parents and children are NOT in the heat of the battle. Consequently, they will buy into just about anything you say if you are not too extreme, harsh, or militant with your seasonal requests and your delivery.

Parent/Player Meeting: Present your preseason parent/player meeting with kindness and respect. Avoid the "drill sergeant" approach that gives off a "do it my way or hit the highway" vibe. That "tough guy" approach wins you nothing but angry parents at the end of your meeting.

Parent/Player Meeting: If there are behavioral suggestions/requirements presented during your meeting, **ALWAYS start with you and your coaches!** Be the good example for everyone.

Practices: Create highly organized practices and keep them short. High-energy and high-tempo practices keep everyone engaged. Get the children in and out, and as good actors would say, "Leave them wanting more." You want your players, when driving home with their parents, saying, *"I can't wait to get back to practice!"*

Showing Respect for EVERYONE: Engage the children with respect and kindness regardless of their age. The tough-guy approach of coaching has come and gone. Today, enlightened coaches recognize that teaching the skills and drills of a sport is no different than teaching in a classroom. Your classroom is your playing field.

Across our country, we are losing officials by the busloads. It has already started, and we will continue to lose many more games because we simply do not have enough officials. Treat **all** officials with respect and become that positive example for your kids, coaches, and parents.

Individual Wins: There are literally hundreds of Individual Wins taking place at every practice and game, and our job, as the coach, is to recognize an Individual Win and reward it.

Individual Wins: Learning how to incorporate Individual Wins into your program requires you to focus on the players' movement and their knowledge of the game and not follow the ball all the time.

That is hard to do, but there is huge payoff for your players and your team!

Creating an Enjoyable Environment: I believe you must make sports a positive and enjoyable experience. If you don't, I can assure you players will quit. Children today have so many other things they can do with their time than attend your practices and games. You are competing for their time and attention. You may not like that, but most children today, for a variety of reasons, are different than you may have been many years ago; good or bad, times have changed.

Field Location: I know we all have GPS and many other digital devices to show you how to get from point A to point B. However, many fields do not have a separate address, and sometimes coaches assume everyone knows where a certain field or facility is; please don't assume anything when it comes to directions. Make sure the parents know exactly where every game field and practice field are located. It is a courtesy thing and takes a lot of pressure off families that are too busy anyway.

Weather: At the youth level, most of you do not have an athletic director giving you direction when it comes to weather, and most of you are not associated with your State High School Association where you have guidelines when it comes to weather. Bottom line, when it comes to various weather conditions, **YOU** are the decision maker. Please err on the side of being overly cautious so that at no time do you put your players, their families, your assistant coaches, or yourself in harm's way. We have no greater responsibility to our children and their families than their safety.

Drop Off and Pick Up: In an earlier chapter, I asked you to be the first to arrive at any practice or game or at least have one coach who can be there before the children arrive. Make sure all children are dropped off safely and, of course, all children are picked up safely. As best you can, please have one adult remain with you until all children have been safely picked up. We have no greater responsibility to our children and their families than their safety.

First Aid: Be prepared for the little hurts and, as best you can, be prepared as to how you will handle a more challenging injury. What is your first aid plan? Do you have ice at every practice and game? Do you have little plastic bags to put ice into in the event you need to apply an ice pack? Do all your players have water, and have you built into your practice and game schedules opportunities to cool down and take a break? Again, we have no greater responsibility to our children and their families than their safety.

CONTINUE TO MAKE YOUR PROGRAM AN EDUCATIONAL AND AN ENJOYABLE EXPERIENCE!

Here are a couple of fun ideas for your kids. Plus, they provide a great learning opportunity.

Softball/Baseball: Starting in about the third or fourth grade, I would prepare a poster board-sized lineup for the players and hang it in a place in the dugout where it was easily visible for all the kids. On one half of the poster board, it had the batting order and where each child played every inning, and on the other half of the poster board, I drew a picture of the field with the positions listed and included any future announcements that the kids and families needed to know about.

Results: I never had to remind the kids where they were in the batting order. I never had to tell them what position they were playing from inning to inning. I never had to explain where second base was or where center field was, and finally, they always knew when and where the next practice or game was going to be.

Bigger Result: The *kids* became more engaged in the game because they were responsible for knowing all that information. A child would ask me when he or she was up to bat, and I would nicely tell them I do not know, but I know where you can go to find that information. In addition, with two outs, my kids would get their gloves, check the poster board lineup, and as soon as the third out occurred, they would run to their position, especially our catcher. Our catcher was always ready!

It took our team about 20 seconds to be on the field and ready to play. I have seen coaches take up to 3 to 4 minutes to get their kids in their on-field positions. If every team did that every inning (let's use 3 minutes over a 7-inning game), it would take some 42 minutes just to get the teams on the field over a 7-inning game. Game time limits will vary depending on the age of the kids. Softball/baseball time limits could be 90 minutes or 120 minutes. If it is a 90-minute time limit, that means 46% of the time, the kids are simply getting positioned on the field and not playing the game. If it is a 120-minute time limit, that means 35% of the time the kids are simply getting positioned on the field and not playing the game. Get creative! Get the kids engaged at a higher level and I guarantee they will enjoy the game more. These kids are smart. They can do this! It made the game more fun!!

Soccer: Starting in about the fifth grade, I put together a soccer playbook for my kids. We had throw-in plays, defensive strategies based on where the ball was, offense strategies based on where the ball was, how to put maximum pressure on an opponent, etc. The kids loved it! When we had a throw-in, the kids, on their own, would yell out colors and our kids would sprint in different directions to throw off their markers. We also had designed "plays" where, on a throw-in, we would throw the ball backward to our defenders, and they would send the ball across the field and up the other side. Most of the time it never worked, but they loved trying it from time to time. It made the game more fun, and it put more responsibility on each player. They had to be engaged! Get the kids engaged at a higher level and I guarantee they will enjoy the game more. These kids are smart. They can do this! It made the game more fun!!

Coaches, get creative and focus on education and fun, and I am highly confident that kids and parents will beat a path to your program from year to year.

Chapter 11

Final Thoughts

Let's summarize: What are you really doing when you say, "Yes, I will coach?" Just like players and their parents, we have a wide range of coaches with varying degrees of skill and experience. Which type of coach are you? Whether you are an experienced coach with a lot of years of coaching or a coach with less than 3 years of coaching experience or you are brand new to coaching, my hope is that you value self-improvement. No matter where you fall on the coaching skill or experience spectrum, you are committed to getting better at your craft (teaching/coaching) from year to year. It doesn't take experience to understand what I have said numerous times in the book, which is, *coaching always comes down to WHO you are and HOW you deliver your program.*

Remember that you are creating a lifetime of memories for these kids and their parents. Will those memories be good memories or unpleasant ones? That is completely up to you.

Please know that the large majority of families you encounter are good families who only want good things for their kids. However, in that quest to take care of their kids, they will step on your toes at times. That doesn't make them bad people. Oftentimes it makes them passionate people who misdirect their passion from time to time. Being aware of this possibility and anticipating bumpy roads leads to developing expectations to smooth out the roads. You will minimize problems, and over time and with experience, you will have very few issues. Why? You got better at your craft.

It's a fact of life that no matter how well you prepare yourself and everyone involved with your team, you may still encounter astonishingly unpleasant people along the way. Just count to ten and calmly deal with them as best you can. If these folks continue to obstruct your program or if they become openly hostile, bring in your organization leaders or your administrative staff. They will help you. You don't have to do everything on your own, especially if you have bent over backwards to help them and the situation.

One more thing about coaching and getting better at your craft from year to year: As an individual, you will become a better person. You will gain additional confidence. You will set new goals for yourself and your team. You will embrace each season as a wonderful opportunity to truly make a positive difference in the lives of your kids, your parents, your assistant coaches, and yourself! And guess what? At no point in this book have I referenced the scoreboard or your final record from year to year as a success factor.

Years ago, I encountered a winless (0-15!) fifth-grade baseball team. When the next season came around, I asked the coach if any kids quit, assuming they wanted to play for a winning team or, at least, a team that could win one or two games. He matter-of-factly said, "They all signed up again for this year." I was incredulous, but he remarked that his players had fun and knew they were playing in a league beyond their skill set. He saw to it that his team was slotted in a more competitive league. It turned out that they were successful on the scoreboard and even advanced to the playoffs. How cool is that? Talk about my new heroes! Even after a winless season, they had made the sporting experience positive enough to bring back every kid and family. That is extraordinary!

Where is your focus? Most people want to be competitive and that is OK, but how you choose to do that is what makes all the difference. I believe you will create a healthier environment if you focus on the individual skills and the enjoyment of that experience as opposed to having a complete focus on the scoreboard.

Keep reminding yourself that you may coach these kids for several years so that you can teach them multiple skills, drills, and strategies of the game over an extended period of time. But this long-term timeline is predicated on having your kids continue to sign up for your sport year after year. One thing is certain: If they do not come out for your sport, you will not be able to teach them anything; they won't be there!

Winning games is a bonus at this level. If you continue to be a better teacher/coach from year to year and your kids continue to learn the keys to competing well in your sport, everyone wins REGARDLESS of what the scoreboard says.

Here is a secret for you: If you are a particularly good teacher/coach and your kids are understanding and learning the game you are teaching, I can almost assure you that you will win more often than you will lose. Better teacher. Better players. Better results. Are you going to win all the time? Probably not. At this level, no matter how well you teach and no matter how well your kids understand the skills, drills, and strategies of the game, you may run into a team with players who are bigger and stronger and more skilled. That happens at this age. All of that starts to even out in junior high and high school.

Bottom line: Forget the scoreboard. Focus on being an effective teacher who creates an enjoyable and challenging experience, and the kids and parents will beat a path to your program from year to year. Coaching always comes down to WHO you are and HOW you deliver your program! Work to become the best at your craft (teaching/coaching)!

Postgame Show/19th Hole/Wrap-Up Show

Coaches, thank you for coaching our children! Without you, we have no programs. As your coaching knowledge and awareness grow, we have much better programs!

Whether you are beginning a new season or wrapping up a season, I hope this book has been a valuable help for you and your program. Coaching has been and always will be about *WHO we are and HOW we deliver our program.*

Very few coaches at this level will ever see one of their players in a professional sports uniform. Some will see a few kids play at the college level, and a few more will smile when they see some of their former athletes play at the high school level. As you are aware, the number of children playing organized sports beyond grade school falls off dramatically and that can be attributed to many factors. My sincere hope for you is that your coaching or your program is not one of those factors.

For a clear majority of the kids, you might be providing the only organized sporting experience of their life. Coaches, though I have already asked a lot of you, I am asking one more thing: Make every practice and every game the best hours of your players' week because of WHO you are and HOW you deliver your program. Someone told me once that most people will not remember every detail of an event or a speech or a situation, but they will always remember how you made them feel!

We want each child to develop a passion for the sport we are coaching. We want to develop players who love coming to practices and games. We want to develop a spirit of cooperation. We want to develop a group of parents who appreciate our goals. We want to develop an understanding of respect. We want to develop a program to which players and parents beat a path to your team because of **WHO you are and HOW you deliver your program**. If wins on the field follow, that is icing on the cake. As best you can, create an environment where all children win regardless of what the scoreboard says.

That is not an easy request, which is why I continually say **thank you** for what you do for our children. Feel good about your choice to coach.

You are a hero!

Coaching is about WHO you are and HOW you deliver your program.

References

References

1. Ewing, Martha E., and Vern Seefeldt. Michigan State University Youth Sports Survey. East Lansing, Mich.: Youth Sports Institute of MSU. The study was reported to the Athletic Footwear Association. Subsequently, additional analysis of the data was performed by Sophisticated Data Research, Inc., of Atlanta. The report was released by the Athletic Footwear Association.

2. Bukatko, Danuta, and Marvin W. Daehler. Child Development: A Thematic Approach. Boston: Houghton Mifflin, pp. 472-74.

3. Harter, S. "The Determinants and Meditational Role of Global Self-worth in Children." In Contemporary Topics in Developmental Psychology, edited by Nancy Eisenberg. New York: Wiley.

4. Dungy, Tony, and Nathan Whitaker. The Mentor Leader: Secrets to Building People and Teams That Win Consistently. Carol Stream, Ill.: Tyndale House, pp. 128-29.

5. Nelson, Jane, Lynn Lott, and H. Stephen Glenn. Positive Discipline in the Classroom: How to Effectively Use Class Meetings and Other Positive Discipline Strategies. Rocklin, Calif.: Prima Publishing, p. 79.